God with all your heart, with all your soul,

d to him, "You shall

ur mind." —Matthew 22:37 Jesus said to h

eart, with all your soul, and with all your min

love the Lord your God with all your heart, w

w 22:37 Jesus said to him, "You shall love

soul, and with all your mind." —Matthew 22

God with all your heart, with all your soul, a

l to him, "You shall love the Lord your God w

ur mind." —Matthew 22:37 Jesus said to h

eart, with all your soul, and with all your mind

love the Lord your God with all your heart, w

w 22:37 Jesus said to him, "You shall love

oul, and with all your mind." —Matthew 22

THE
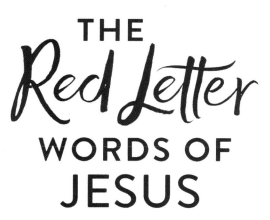
Red Letter
WORDS OF
JESUS

JACK COUNTRYMAN

Published in Nashville, Tennessee, by Thomas Nelson. Thomas
Nelson is a registered trademark of HarperCollins Christian
Publishing, Inc.

Unless otherwise noted, Scripture quotations are taken from the
New King James Version®. © 1982 by Thomas Nelson. Used by
permission. All rights reserved.

Cover design by Thinkpen Design
Interior design by Kristy L. Edwards

ISBN 978-0-7180-9699-1

Printed in China
17 18 19 20 21 DSC 5 4 3 2 1

THE

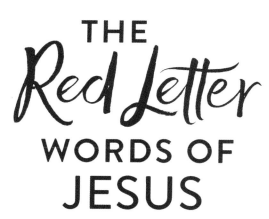

WORDS OF
JESUS

JACK COUNTRYMAN

A Division of Thomas Nelson Publishers

THOMAS NELSON
Since 1798

Introduction

As far back as I can remember, I have been fascinated with the words Jesus spoke. His conversations with His disciples, His answers to the Pharisees' often trick questions, what He said when He performed His miracles, the penetrating, compelling statements in His teachings—even today all these words Jesus spoke continue to draw men and women to Him. The Gospels are filled with Jesus' words, parables, and sermons. In a message consistent in all four Gospels, Jesus shows us the way to be saved, calls us to follow Him, and invites us to know rest and peace in His presence.

Louis Klopsch (1852–1910) is credited with the idea of printing Jesus' words in red. The editor of the *Christian Herald* magazine, Klopsch came up with the idea of printing some of the biblical text with red ink while he was reading Jesus' words, "This cup is the new covenant in My blood, which is shed for you" (Luke 22:20). Klopsch decided to print all of Jesus' words in red, the

color of His blood. The first red-letter New Testament was printed in 1899, and the first red-letter Bible was printed in 1901 ("Origin of Red-Letter Bibles," *Crossway*. March 23, 2006. https://www.crossway.org/blog/2006/03/red-letter-origin/).

In this book, *The Red Letter Words of Jesus*, I have chosen more than one hundred passages that reveal Jesus' divine nature, His servanthood, and His love for all humankind. Jesus is the Giver of life, and in Him we can rest and be secure. Knowing Jesus through His words gives significance to our years on this earth and a peace that passes all understanding.

MAN SHALL NOT

LIVE

BY BREAD ALONE,
BUT BY EVERY WORD
THAT PROCEEDS
FROM THE MOUTH OF

GOD.

— MATTHEW 4:4 —

Before Jesus began His earthly ministry, the Spirit led Him into the wilderness where He would be tempted by the devil. After Jesus had fasted for forty days and forty nights, Satan challenged Him to turn the desert rocks into bread, to meet His needs in His own time and His own way, without considering God's timing or ways. But when Jesus faced the temptation to create bread for Himself—and just as in the two subsequent wilderness temptations—Jesus responded to Satan's words with the powerful words of God. Each time Jesus began with "It is written," and each time Jesus quoted God's truth and silenced the enemy. Jesus knew that God would provide the needed food at the right time.

Christians must know what God's Word says. They also must be willing to trust His timing. When you choose to build your life on His Word, you can—as Jesus did—stand strong against any temptation you find yourself facing. You can also trust Him to provide for you according to His perfect will. Follow Jesus' example and confront every temptation with "It is written." You will find strength in God's true Word and the faith to trust in His timing.

FOR IT IS WRITTEN,

"You shall *worship* the Lord your God, and Him only you shall serve."

MATTHEW 4:10

During Jesus' time in the wilderness, Satan tempted Jesus by offering Him all the kingdoms of the world . . . *if* Jesus would fall down and worship him. Turning to God's Word and allowing it to guide His choice, Jesus said, "It is written." Jesus spoke aloud God's command—"You shall worship the LORD your God"—thereby ending His conversation with Satan. Jesus had overcome all of Satan's temptations by quoting the Scriptures.

Consider the items you are tempted to worship. The list of items that come to mind may seem full of clichés, but try not to dismiss them. Each one has the ability to attract your worship. What does the world invite you to worship? The world encourages you to set up an altar to—among other things—self, family, money, possessions, and status. When one of those temptations beckons you, try to follow Jesus' example. Choose to say aloud and boldly, "It is written, 'You shall worship the LORD your God, and Him only you shall serve.'" Trust that the temptation will abate just as it did in Jesus' case.

Then He said to them,

"Follow Me,

AND I WILL MAKE YOU
FISHERS OF MEN."

MATTHEW 4:19

After His temptations with Satan ended, Jesus began His earthly ministry. While Jesus walked by the Sea of Galilee, He came upon two brothers, Simon Peter and Andrew. He did not beg them to follow Him or make great promises about what the future with Him held. Jesus simply said, "Follow Me, and I will make you fishers of men." The two brothers immediately dropped what they were doing and began to follow Jesus.

Today Jesus calls you to follow Him, to drop your old way of life and live as He models and teaches you to live. When you choose to follow Him, the relationship you forge with Jesus will give your life meaning and purpose.

God gives everyone certain talents and gifts that He wants him or her to use for His glory. He also uses Christians when they willingly surrender their lives to Him. When you do this day in and day out, you will experience a richness and joy as you live with His Spirit alive in your heart. What greater blessing could you ever ask for? The Lord calls you today. Will you follow Him?

BLESSED ARE THE PURE IN HEART, FOR THEY SHALL SEE GOD.

MATTHEW 5:8

The first verses of Matthew 5 list the Beatitudes, which were blessings spoken by Jesus for His followers. In verse eight, Jesus said, "Blessed are the pure in heart, for they shall see God." So can flawed, imperfect people ever be pure in heart? Yes they can, but they will only be pure in heart if God purifies their hearts—and, thankfully, God can do that.

Your heart is purified when you put your faith in the truth that Jesus is God's Son, when you believe the blood He shed on the cross paid the price for your sins, and when you believe that He rose from the dead, victorious over sin and death. This does not mean you will never sin again while on earth, so how do you keep your heart pure? Again, you can't on your own, but God can when you ask: "Create in me a clean heart, O God" (Psalm 51:10). Purified by God, you see God, just as Jesus promised. You have access to your holy Father, and you can fellowship with Him through the privilege of prayer. Furthermore, you will one day see God face-to-face in heaven.

YOU ARE THE SALT OF THE EARTH

MATTHEW 5:13

Jesus told His followers they were the salt of the earth. This was an obvious metaphor for how they should impact the world around them. Salt has many different uses. First, salt preserves food. Before refrigeration, people salted foods, which made them last significantly longer than they did when left unsalted. Salt also adds flavor to foods. Many foods would be bland and—to some—inedible without salt. So adding salt makes dishes more palatable.

What does it mean when Jesus calls you to be the salt of the earth? Jesus uses those who love and follow Him to help preserve this fallen world that has turned its back on Him. Jesus also uses you to spread the Word in a way that is easier for others to understand, easier for them to hear and digest, by adding flavor and depth to your words as you share the gospel. Salt brings out distinct flavors in food, just as believers can bring out the words of God to impact listeners in a positive way. Those who know Jesus, radiate His joy, and share His love add flavor to the world. Look for ways today to be the salt of the earth in your words and actions.

LET YOUR
LIGHT
SO SHINE
BEFORE MEN,
THAT THEY MAY SEE
YOUR GOOD WORKS

and glorify
YOUR FATHER IN HEAVEN.

MATTHEW 5:16

A little bit of light impacts a lot of darkness. The inky blackness of a cave is not so ominous once you turn on a flashlight. Light also gives comfort throughout the night—the literal night as well as the metaphorical night. And light—the sun bursting through the rainclouds— brings hope and joy with each new day.

This is why Jesus called for His followers to let their lights "shine before men." Those who have named Jesus as Savior and Lord have the ability to shine this kind of comforting, joyful light to people in the world. Do you know that within you is a light burning with heaven's fire? As a result, your faith should cause you to behave differently than the world. Your true faith in God should show through in your actions and reflect your heavenly Father. People should see God through you.

When you walk with God, His Spirit shines your light before others so people see your good works and the love of God within you. God has given you the gift of light within you. May you use it for His glory. After all, a little bit of light dispels a lot of darkness.

Whoever **compels** you to go one mile, go with him **two.**

Matthew 5:41

Throughout the Sermon on the Mount, Jesus offered straightforward and radical instructions for His followers—among them: "agree with your adversary quickly"; don't "resist an evil person. . . . whoever slaps you on your right cheek, turn the other to him also"; and "whoever compels you to go one mile, go with him two" (Matthew 5:25, 39, 41). Such instructions would have puzzled His listeners.

Jesus summarized these sayings with the commands, "Love your enemies, bless those who curse you, [and] do good to those who hate you" (v. 44). In Jesus' day, the Romans were the Jews' enemies and oppressors. The Romans could force Jews, randomly chosen along the road, to carry whatever needed to be carried. Yet Jesus told His listeners to love these enemies by carrying the load not just for one mile but for two miles.

Be aware of times when you could stop—figuratively speaking—at one mile when asked to help someone. Take a minute to consider going a second mile, knowing the difference a little extra work will make, especially if you help someone with whom you don't get along.

For if you *love* those who love you,
what reward have you?

MATTHEW 5:46

People who love Jesus are supposed to act differently than those who don't. They should have different activities on Sunday morning, different ways to spend their money, a different perspective on current events, and a compassion and peace that perplexes the world. But the temptation to blend in with the culture and remain silent about faith can be quite strong at times.

Maybe people will know you by your love for others, but as Jesus pointed out in His Sermon on the Mount, there is nothing remarkable about your love if you only love people who love you in return. Yet Jesus' command was to "love your enemies" (v. 44). And He continued: "Bless those who curse you, do good to those who hate you, and pray for those who spitefully use you" (v. 44). You should be known for the love you show to those who treat you poorly.

Who has hurt you, cursed you, or used you? What will loving those people require of your actions and words? Choose one of those people to love this week. Start with a small step—and know that God will smile on your obedience.

TAKE HEED

THAT YOU ⟵————————

DO NOT DO YOUR

charitable DEEDS

BEFORE MEN, TO BE

————⟶ SEEN BY THEM.

MATTHEW 6:1

Why do we serve at the soup kitchen, teach the two-year-olds every Sunday morning, lead a midweek Bible study, or volunteer at the Red Cross? We do good works and serve others to please the Lord. He is the one we long to please, and when He is pleased with us, we experience joy as we sense His approval.

The world sometimes notices what you do for the Lord and offers affirmation and appreciation for your services. For example, the Pharisees in Jesus' days loved to be praised by men for their good works. But you are to receive such recognition humbly—and, as Jesus taught in Matthew 6, not allow the desire for such recognition to motivate your service. Jesus said those who perform good deeds in secret will be recognized by the Father and rewarded openly. The world's praise of your "charitable deeds" is fleeting, but the Father's reward for your service is eternal.

May the giving of your time, money, and talents for the Lord and His purposes bring you the heartfelt satisfaction of knowing you are pleasing the Lord rather than the world.

OUR FATHER IN
HEAVEN,
HALLOWED BE YOUR NAME.
YOUR KINGDOM COME.
YOUR WILL BE DONE ON EARTH AS IT IS IN HEAVEN.
GIVE US THIS DAY OUR DAILY BREAD.
AND FORGIVE US OUR DEBTS, AS WE FORGIVE OUR DEBTORS.
AND DO NOT LEAD US
INTO TEMPTATION,
BUT DELIVER US
FROM THE EVIL ONE.
FOR YOURS IS THE
KINGDOM
AND THE POWER
AND THE GLORY
FOREVER.
AMEN.
MATTHEW 6:9–13

In Matthew 6, Jesus taught His disciples a model prayer to aid their prayer time with God. The Lord's Prayer is a wonderful example for all disciples to follow when they find themselves struggling to pray.

The Lord's Prayer starts by your giving honor to God as well as praying for His perfect will to be done on earth. After this, pray for your personal needs, asking God to provide the essentials for your existence (food, shelter, and clothing). Your heart is important to God, too, which is why you also must ask Him to forgive your sins and enable you to forgive those who have hurt you. Next, ask God to protect you from temptation and from the deceit of the evil one.

Communicating with the Lord is not about speaking the right words or finding the most effective formula to please God. Prayer is about communicating from the heart and being open and honest with the God of the universe. If you follow the Lord's Prayer, then you will be able to deepen your communication with Him.

FOR WHERE
your TREASURE IS,
THERE YOUR

Heart

WILL BE ALSO.

MATTHEW 6:21

What do you desire above all else? Is it success, wealth, recognition, or the perfect family? Everyone has certain ambitions in life, and achieving them can bring prestige in the eyes of the world.

But in Matthew 6 Jesus commanded: "Do not lay up for yourselves treasures on earth" (v. 19). Instead Christians are to "lay up . . . treasures in heaven" (v. 20). Nothing can steal your heavenly treasures. Moth and rust and time itself can destroy earthly treasures you strive to accumulate, but treasure you accumulate as you live for the Lord will last forever in heaven.

Your heart—your desires, your feelings, and your beliefs—will follow your treasures. Storing up heavenly treasures ensures a heart full of the joy God wants for you now on earth. But this path is not an easy path; temptations and pressures to find success in the world can seem quicker and easier than this path. Remember that God promises to provide all you need for this life, and God always keeps His promises. So, focus on storing up treasures in heaven for your eternal good and His glory!

No one can serve

2

MASTERS. . . .

You cannot serve God and mammon.

MATTHEW 6:24

God generously gives you the freedom to make many choices in your life. The primary choice that impacts all the others, though, is the choice of whom you will serve.

Matthew 6:24 reminds Christians that God will not be second in their lives. If you want to please Him, He must be first in your life. You must to choose to walk with Him and to live in His presence. Even though His presence includes purpose, joy, love, and peace, the world's beckoning voice still can be alluring and the love of money strongly tempting. Yet Jesus said you cannot serve two masters because you "will hate the one and love the other, or . . . be loyal to the one and despise the other" (v. 24). Either God will be first in your life or something else will be. The choice is up to you.

When choosing whom you will serve, remember that God wants to have a relationship with you. When you choose to put Him first in your life, the attractions of this world will become less appealing. Living for God's glory will be the most important aspect of your life.

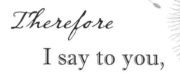

Therefore

I say to you,

DO NOT

WORRY

about your life.

Matthew 6:25

Have you ever noticed that the command "do not worry about your life" comes immediately after Jesus said "you cannot serve God and mammon" (v. 24)? After all, where is your trust—in God or in mammon—when you worry about having what you need in this life? You are not trusting God when you are worrying.

Be encouraged about what Jesus said shortly after this command not to worry. He reminded His disciples God cares for even the least in creation, the birds of the air and the lilies of the field, so surely God would care to a greater degree for His followers. Instead of worrying about basic necessities, His followers should focus their attention on deepening their relationship with God.

God will provide for you, regardless of the person, relationship, or situation that causes you concern. He will give you a clear awareness of His provision today, as well as vivid memories of how He has provided for you in years past. There is no time for worrying if you truly trust God.

SEEK FIRST

THE **KINGDOM** OF

GOD

AND HIS

righteousness,

AND ALL THESE THINGS

SHALL BE ADDED
TO YOU.

MATTHEW 6:33

Earlier in Matthew 6, Jesus said not to worry about what you will eat and drink and wear—your everyday essentials. If God cares for even the least in creation, then He cares for you exponentially more. At the same time, Jesus didn't tell you to stop worrying about food, shelter, or clothing because you don't really need them. Rather, Jesus encouraged you not to worry about such matters but instead to focus on the truths that God is in charge of your life and He will take care of you.

Jesus encouraged you to seek first His kingdom and His righteousness and let Him take care of the food, drink, and clothing you need. This means living in a way that will serve and honor Him. If you focus on doing this, you will stop worrying about whether or not you will go without the basic necessities.

God promises to take care of the essentials, freeing you to live a fruitful life for His glory. Shift your focus from your worries and onto God, and your eyes will be opened to see how much He provides for you every day.

Ask,

AND IT WILL BE GIVEN TO YOU;

seek,

AND YOU WILL FIND;

knock,

AND IT WILL BE OPENED TO YOU.

MATTHEW 7:7

You often keep your personal life separate from your work life. But when you develop a relationship with God, He does not want to be restricted to just one specific area of your life. He wants to be involved in your life from the moment you awaken until you fall asleep at night. He wants you to seek Him with purpose and to persevere in your pursuit of Him. He does this because, as your heavenly Father, He loves you and wants to provide for you.

God truly does want to be included in every aspect of your life. So in Matthew 7:7, Jesus invited you to share with the Lord what you are thinking, to ask humbly for what you want, to seek Him for solutions to problems, and to knock—to persevere in prayer—so He can bless you with what He knows is best for you.

This invitation from the Lord to ask, seek, and knock reflects His desire to be involved in your life for your good and His glory. As your heavenly Father, He wants to bestow love and blessings in every area of your life.

Therefore whoever hears these sayings of Mine, and does them, I will liken him to a *wise* man who built his house on the **ROCK**.

MATTHEW 7:24

Jesus concluded the Sermon on the Mount by making it clear to His listeners that the choice was theirs: Would they decide to follow Him and His teachings, or would they ignore Him and continue with their own worldly thinking? A decision to follow Jesus' teachings would result in receiving His blessings.

Jesus offered a word picture that warned about the consequences of building their lives on an improper foundation. First, the better option: building a life on Jesus' teachings is like building a house on a solid rock. Followers of Jesus will be able to stand strong in their faith no matter what storms of life come their way. In sharp contrast is the second option: building your life on what the world values is like building a house on sand. The rain, floods, and winds of life will cause the walls to crumble and fall. The house will be destroyed.

Jesus' question to His listeners is also presented to you: Will you allow Him to serve as the rock for your life, or will you choose a different foundation?

The

HARVEST TRULY IS PLENTIFUL,

but the laborers

ARE FEW.

MATTHEW 9:37

Jesus traveled to many towns and villages during His earthly ministry, and He encountered many different kinds of people with various kinds of problems. Matthew 9:36 says that when Jesus saw these people, He felt profound compassion for them because He knew they were lost "like sheep having no shepherd." Jesus knew His listening crowd needed to hear about God's love if they were going to live an abundant life on earth and spend eternity with their heavenly Father. Thus, Jesus pointed out to His disciples this responsibility to serve Him by introducing people to the truth of God's love.

Jesus gave you the same command to share the gospel, to speak confidently about your relationship with Him, and to be bold in presenting why everyone is in need of a Savior. Ask God to give you the courage to share your love for Jesus, to be a laborer for the gospel. Then trust the Holy Spirit will enable you to share what it means to walk hand in hand with the One who gave His life so all men and women can experience God's love and have life everlasting.

For
it is not you
WHO SPEAK,
but the *Spirit*
of your FATHER
who speaks
in you.

MATTHEW 10:20

No one wants to be persecuted for his or her beliefs. Yet in this broken world of darkness and sin, the choice to stand for truth and light—to speak of God and to name Jesus as Lord—will bring persecution. That was as true in Jesus' day as it is today, and Jesus addressed the matter.

In Matthew 10, Jesus chose the twelve disciples and commissioned them to take the gospel to the Jews. Along with this commissioning, Jesus warned they would face severe persecution. Understandably, men who had previously been fishermen or other modest occupations might have felt intimidated. Would their defense of their faith be articulate and accurate? In like manner, many believers today worry their words won't be good enough, so they never share their faith with anyone.

But Jesus told His disciples, "It is not you who speak, but the Spirit . . . who speaks in you." When you want to take a stand for truth, call on the Holy Spirit and trust Him to provide help. As Jesus promised, what you need to say "will be given to you in that hour" (v. 19). When the time comes, God will give you the words to say and the strength you need.

Whatever
I tell you
in the DARK,
speak in the
light.

Matthew 10:27

Different seasons call for different strategies. Earlier in His ministry, Jesus often told others to keep His identity a secret. But the time had come for a different strategy. The season of proclaiming the truth about His identity had arrived.

This passage continues Jesus' commissioning of the twelve disciples. He again warned them of the persecution that would result from sharing the gospel. But Jesus said, "Do not fear" because enemies of the gospel could kill only the body, not the soul (v. 28). Then Jesus reminded His disciples of their great value to God and the fact that He would be with them at all times. Therefore, they needed to preach the gospel in the light and from the rooftops no matter what.

Christians today should also stay alert for Satan, who prowls like a lion looking for its prey. In spite of this, be mindful that—with your behavior as well as your words—you are God's ambassador. He wants you to share the truth of the gospel boldly and without fear. Ask God to give you the courage to let your light shine so people may see Christ in the world.

Whoever
CONFESSES Me
before men, him
I will also CONFESS
before My Father
who is in heaven.

Matthew 10:32

When we hear the word *confess*, we often think of admitting our sins, and that is one meaning of *confess*. But here in the context of Jesus' talking to His twelve disciples, *confess* means to declare one's allegiance to someone or something.

Whenever someone takes a public stand for the gospel, Jesus will tell His Father of this person's loyalty and faith. Taking such an unwavering stand for Jesus, though, is not easy in the face of persecution. Simply denying any connection with Jesus may be all it takes to avoid persecution. But as Jesus warned: "Whoever denies Me before men, him I will also deny before My Father who is in heaven" (v. 33). Thus, Jesus' warning was clear: if someone denies knowing Jesus while on earth, then Jesus will deny knowing this person on the Day of Judgment.

If you're concerned about your ability to stand strong in the face of persecution, look back at Jesus' promise in Matthew 10:20. The Spirit will speak through you for your good and for God's glory. Ask God to give you the boldness needed to confess allegiance to Jesus when times of persecution arise.

HE WHO

FINDS

HIS LIFE

WILL LOSE IT,

AND HE WHO LOSES

HIS LIFE

FOR MY SAKE

will find it.

Matthew 10:39

This verse is a paradox because a truth is found in an obvious contradiction. How can one lose his life and find it, whereas one who saves his life will lose it? Isn't this physically impossible? But Jesus made it clear: the person who deems his life in this world to be supremely important and who makes living for the world his total focus will lose the eternal life that Jesus offers. In contrast, the person who does not spend his life chasing after all that the world offers—and who thereby loses his life as the world defines it—will find and experience eternal life with God. Upon closer examination, the truth of the paradox becomes clear.

The promise of eternal life is yours the minute you accept Jesus as Savior and Lord. With your focus on Him and your heart overflowing with His love, you can lose yourself in your pursuit of God and what matters for eternal life. And that, Jesus taught, is the far better option.

Come to *Me,* **all**
you who labor
and are heavy
& laden,
I will
give you
rest.

MATTHEW 11:28

When Jesus spoke these words, He addressed people weighed down by the crushing burden of Jewish legalism who were laboring to earn their way to heaven by keeping the strict man-made laws enforced by the scribes and Pharisees. Since keeping the law of Moses demanded perfection, they had no hope of ever finding relief. Imagine how they must have felt when they heard this invitation from Jesus.

The Lord extends this same invitation to you today. Jesus invites you to come to Him with your physical, as well as, your spiritual weariness, and He promises to give you rest. He offers you His yoke, so you may learn from Him as He leads. Next, Jesus promises rest for your soul. Jesus feels compassion for you and offers you hope and freedom from burdens, especially those weighing you down spiritually. He beckons you to come to Him and find rest for your soul.

What concerns are weighing you down right now? No Christian should feel he or she must shoulder the load alone. Cast your burden on Jesus, and let Him give you the rest you seek.

For the *Son of Man* is LORD even of the SABBATH.

MATTHEW 12:8

The Jewish leaders esteemed God's law and knew it well. They also had added many extra laws to ensure faithful followers would not accidentally violate God's commands, such as His command that the Sabbath be a day of rest.

Matthew 12 opens with Jesus and His disciples walking through grain fields on the Sabbath. The disciples were hungry, so they plucked heads of grain and ate them. When the Pharisees saw this, they went to Jesus and argued that no one should ever work on the Sabbath, even if they were hungry. In response to this, Jesus offered a different interpretation of the Sabbath law. He reminded the Pharisees of how David had eaten of the bread from the temple (which was forbidden by the law) when he was hungry, yet God did not hold it against him because David had good reason to do so.

God commanded His people to rest on the Sabbath for their good, and Jesus restored that focus. Trying to follow meaningless regulations did not help anyone. Ask God to give you wisdom in discerning the best way to honor the Sabbath.

WHOEVER DOES
THE WILL OF
MY FATHER
IN HEAVEN
IS MY *brother*
AND
sister
AND
mother.

MATTHEW 12:50

While Jesus was teaching a multitude, someone told Jesus that His mother, Mary, and His brothers wanted to speak to Him. Instead of going outside to meet his family, Jesus responded with the question, "Who is My mother and who are My brothers?" (v. 48). Jesus took this opportunity to communicate that His role as God's Son, the spotless Lamb who would die for the forgiveness of humanity's sin, took priority over spending time with His earthly family. Jesus then pointed out that those who were faithful to God's will were now His true family members.

Jesus' calling to serve His heavenly Father and His will was His primary responsibility while He was on earth. The same is true for Jesus' followers now. Of course, biological families remain important, but individuals who choose to commit their lives to serving the Lord and doing God's will are—as Jesus put it—His brother, sister, and mother.

Take a moment to consider the members of your family. Thank God for them, but also thank God for adopting you into His family, which is far more important.

THE

kingdom

heaven

OF

IS LIKE

treasure

HIDDEN IN A FIELD.

MATTHEW 13:44

Jesus often spoke in parables to teach a lesson to His hearers. The parables often used everyday examples to which His audience could relate. The parable Jesus told in today's verse addresses what Christians must be willing to sacrifice for God. Jesus told of a man who found a treasure which had been hidden in a field. The man, with great joy, then went and sold all he had so he could buy the field.

In this parable, the treasure represents God's kingdom. The man, having found the Lord, willingly gave away everything he owned just so he could have the treasure that is the Lord. Clearly, the man recognized the value of God's kingdom as well as the life-changing opportunity he had right in front of him. He knew what needed to be done, and he put his plan into action without hesitation.

This is a powerful picture for Christians today. Are you willing to sell all you have—to pour all of your time and resources into God's kingdom? His kingdom is priceless and offers eternal reward. Like the man in Jesus' story, strive to invest with great joy everything in God's kingdom.

IF
ANYONE
DESIRES
TO COME
AFTER ME,
LET HIM
DENY HIMSELF,
AND TAKE UP

HIS CROSS,
AND FOLLOW
Me.

MATTHEW 16:24

Crucifixion was a brutal and excruciatingly painful way to die, and the Romans perfected it. The person nailed to the cross grew weak from loss of blood from the puncture wounds, yet in order to breathe, he needed to lift himself up with his arms and push himself up with feet that had been pierced by nails. The effort was exhausting; the eventual result was death by suffocation.

Yet this is the metaphor Jesus used when He spoke of living a life committed to Him. This striking image communicates the dying to self that Jesus modeled and called His disciples to emulate. While on earth Jesus submitted to the will of the Father, and we should as well. When we name Jesus as our Savior and Lord, when we answer His call to follow Him, His will for our lives becomes more important than our desires. We must be willing to sacrifice everything to follow Him.

The Christian life does not promise a trouble-free existence, but Jesus will give you not only the strength to endure whatever comes your way, but also the grace of His presence to sustain you.

IF YOU HAVE

faith

AS A MUSTARD SEED,

YOU WILL SAY TO THIS

MOUNTAIN,

"Move from here to there,"

AND IT WILL MOVE.

MATTHEW 17:20

Faith is essential to being a Christian. Trusting that God will forgive your sins, provide for your needs, and give you eternal life is part of what it means to be a Christ follower. Yet not everyone has the same amount of faith in God all the time.

Jesus told His disciples if they had faith the size of a mustard seed, then they could move mountains. The metaphor used by Jesus was an idea known in Jewish literature, so His audience would have been familiar with the concept. When Jesus used the image, it was a picture of the seemingly impossible. Yet with God all things are possible. Jesus recognized the weak faith of His disciples and used this image to challenge them to exercise what little faith they had, knowing their faith would increase as they saw God come through for them.

Your trust in God deepens when you choose to trust Him and depend on Him. Keeping a record of those times when God has come through for you will help your faith grow deeper and stronger. What mountains have you seen God move in your life?

Whoever
humbles himself
as this little child
is the greatest
in the kingdom of
HEAVEN.

Matthew 18:4

Jesus stressed the importance of humility throughout His ministry. Humility means not thinking too highly—or even too frequently—of yourself. One way to maintain an accurate perspective of yourself is to keep looking up to God, the Creator and Sustainer of life. Seeing the mountains, the oceans, or the stars can help you appreciate the majesty and magnitude of God's power. At the same time, you will recognize the minuscule power you possess.

Jesus said if you want to reach the kingdom of heaven, then you must go before God as a child. Children often have more faith than adults because they aren't as jaded by the world and those who might have disappointed them in times past. In like manner, you need to have faith in Him and learn from Him with a childlike heart that is open and trusting.

Children are willing to trust until they're taught not to trust. Your trustworthy God is completely faithful not only to His promises but also to His holy and compassionate nature. Your humble, childlike faith in God will never be misplaced because He will never let you down.

Where two or three
are gathered together in

My name,
I am there

in the midst of them.

Matthew 18:20

Later in Matthew 19 a rich young ruler approached Jesus and asked what he needed to do to gain eternal life. The young man was proud of the fact he had kept the commandments since childhood, and he was sure he was in God's good graces. Yet Jesus told the young man to sell all his possessions, give the proceeds to the poor, and then follow Him. Unfortunately, the rich young ruler left Jesus saddened by the fact he had to give up his possessions.

The way to attain eternal life is to heed Jesus' call to follow Him at all costs. Your positive response to that call will mean spiritual satisfaction, but your denial of the call will lead to spiritual emptiness. You can respond to Jesus and receive joy, but if you ignore Jesus you will continue to seek spiritual satisfaction.

Think of what you have had to give up to follow Jesus. As you can attest, the reward far exceeds the cost. When you follow Jesus, you are in the relationship God created you to be in. You come alive spiritually when you choose to follow Jesus, and you experience blessings as you walk hand in hand with Christ as your Lord.

IT IS EASIER FOR A CAMEL
TO GO THROUGH THE
EYE OF A NEEDLE
THAN FOR A RICH MAN
TO ENTER THE
KINGDOM OF
God.

MATTHEW 19:24

Today's passage follows Jesus' encounter with the rich young ruler. After the young man departed, Jesus used strong hyperbole to express the difficulty rich people have in gaining eternal life. This does not mean rich people cannot go to heaven. People such as Abraham, David, and Solomon were wealthy because God greatly blessed them. At the same time, Jesus knew those who are extremely comfortable in this world often do not see their need for God.

Most people battle with the desire and even the natural tendency to be independent and self-reliant. At the root of that desire, however, can be a sense of pride and the belief that one can be successful without God's help. Fueling this sense of self-reliance can be a full bank account and a lucrative career, which can sometimes bring people to the false conclusion they do not need God in their lives—until they reach a crisis.

Jesus understood wealth can be a distraction, and He wants you to keep your attention on Him so your trust is in Him and not in the comforts of the world.

JUST AS THE

SON OF MAN

DID NOT COME TO BE SERVED,

BUT TO

SERVE,

AND TO

GIVE HIS LIFE

A RANSOM FOR MANY.

MATTHEW 20:28

The mother of James and John came to Jesus and requested that her sons be granted the positions of sitting on Jesus' right and left hand in His kingdom. This request upset the other ten disciples, which led to the discourse on servanthood found in this chapter of Matthew.

If serving is below you, leadership is beyond you. This statement reflects the principle Jesus Christ lived and taught: servant leadership. If someone wants to be a good leader, then he or she must be a humble servant.

Jesus is the King of kings and Lord of lords, yet He came to this earth to serve. That service took on many different forms—from teaching and healing to giving up His life as the sinless Lamb of God. Jesus did not exercise His authority by overruling the Jewish officials or Roman soldiers who opposed Him, nor did He choose His way over God's will. Instead, Jesus went to the cross, where His ultimate act of service and love saved our souls and glorified God.

If you want to imitate Jesus, then be a servant to others.

YOU SHALL *love* THE
LORD YOUR GOD
WITH ALL YOUR *heart,*
WITH ALL YOUR *soul,*
AND WITH ALL YOUR *mind.* MATTHEW 22:37

A lawyer once approached Jesus and asked which was the greatest commandant in the Law of Moses. Jesus answered with the key verse for today's devotion. This commandment and the one that follows it—"You shall love your neighbor as yourself" (v. 39)—summarize the Ten Commandments as well as the rest of the Law and Prophets.

Jesus commanded you to love God with all of your heart, soul, and mind, which means your entire being should be devoted to Him. It is a command to put God first and foremost in everything you say and do. Loving God means allowing Him to guide you and honoring Him with your every thought, word, and action.

You are also to honor God by your obedience to the second commandment as well. You are to treat your neighbors as you want to be treated—with love, kindness, thoughtfulness, and courtesy. When you live this way—with God's help—you reflect the love of Jesus to others.

HOW OFTEN
I WANTED TO
GATHER

YOUR CHILDREN
TOGETHER, AS A HEN
GATHERS HER CHICKS
UNDER HER WINGS.

MATTHEW 23:37

Today's passage continues Jesus' teachings known as the Olivet Discourse. Jesus said one day He will be coming back "on the clouds of heaven" (v. 30), but no one knows when this will happen—not even the Son of Man. (This doesn't take away from Jesus' omniscience; rather, only the Father is the One who does know.) Despite many attempts over the centuries to pinpoint the time of Jesus' return, the words of Jesus remain true: He will come at an hour no one expects. Christians are, therefore, to remain in a perpetual state of readiness, making sure the lives they lead glorify God.

Too often, however, believers let emotions, pleasures, and responsibilities take control of their lives, and their relationship with God becomes a low priority. Yet Christians are to live with anticipation of that glorious day as well as an urgency to share the gospel with people who aren't ready for Jesus' return.

Do you live in expectation of Christ's return? If so, then your life's priorities have changed from what they were before you came to expect His coming. Ask God to keep you alert and ready for Jesus' imminent return.

Well done,
GOOD AND
FAITHFUL
SERVANT.

MATTHEW 25:21

Jesus told a parable about a master who entrusted talents to his servants. He gave five talents to one servant, two talents to a second servant, and one talent to a third servant. The master went on a journey and returned to see what his servants had done with the money. He found the first two servants had invested their money and made a profit, but the third servant had hidden the money in a hole in the ground. The master praised the first two servants but punished the third servant because he had not put the talent to good use.

Jesus made clear God gives everyone different "talents," or responsibilities, in His kingdom. God also assigns varying degrees of responsibility because He knows what we can handle. How we choose to handle the gifts God gives us—what we do as stewards of the time, money, and skills He entrusts to our care—will determine whether or not one day we hear: "Well done, good and faithful servant."

Think about the talents God has given to you. Ask the Holy Spirit to help you be a better steward of these talents, so you can be a faithful servant of God.

Watch *and* pray,
LEST YOU ENTER INTO
TEMPTATION.
THE *spirit* INDEED
IS WILLING,
||||| ► B · U · T ◄ |||||
THE FLESH IS WEAK.

Matthew 26:41

Jesus and His disciples were in the Garden of Gethsemane prior to Jesus' arrest. Wanting to spend some time alone in prayer, Jesus spoke these words to His disciples before leaving them. While alone, He asked His Father not to make Him endure the planned crucifixion. This gave the disciples the opportunity to support Jesus with prayer. Yet three times Jesus returned from praying and found them asleep. When Jesus needed their support, they had failed Him.

Jesus' words ring true today for His followers. Christians should be alert at all times because "the devil walks about like a roaring lion, seeking whom he may devour" (1 Peter 5:8). Being vigilant and watching for temptation is wise for all Christians.

Christians are also to stay in a constant mindset of prayer, which Paul speaks of in 1 Thessalonians 5:17. If Christians stay in consistent communion with God, then they will keep themselves from temptation.

Keep alert and pray often, regardless of your circumstances or how you are feeling.

GO therefore & MAKE DISCIPLES of all the nations.

MATTHEW 28:19

The Gospel of Matthew closes with a direct call to action. Just prior to His ascension, Jesus met with the remaining eleven disciples. He told them to go into all the world and make disciples. Jesus then promised to be with them every step as they spread the gospel.

God wants you to share with others the blessings He has bestowed upon you. And the Great Commission is a perfect example of that pattern. You are to make disciples of all nations, and you can confidently go forward on this assignment under the divine authority of Jesus.

Your job is to be a faithful messenger of the truth about Jesus—His death, His resurrection, His love, His teachings, His commands, and His eternal reign. God will work in the hearts of the people with whom you share the gospel. The convicting power of the Holy Spirit will bring them to repentance and salvation.

God will also give you the necessary strength and courage to spread the gospel. You never need to worry that you are alone in sharing the good news. He will be with you wherever you go and help you make disciples of all nations.

Jesus came to Galilee
. . . saying,

"THE KINGDOM OF GOD IS

AT HAND.

REPENT, AND BELIEVE IN THE

GOSPEL."

MARK 1:14–15

The Gospel of Mark opens at a rapid pace. In the first thirteen verses, Mark covers the ministry of John the Baptist, Jesus' baptism, and Jesus' temptation in the wilderness. Following this, Mark writes how Jesus began His ministry and went to Galilee, "preaching the gospel of the kingdom of God" (v. 14). Jesus' message was for all to repent and believe in the gospel. Jesus' call is the same today. He wants people to repent of their sins, believe He is the Son of God, receive the blessings of the Holy Spirit, and obtain life everlasting with the Father.

To repent means that you will turn from sin and dedicate yourself to changing your life. This is more than just a feeling of regret. This is about realizing your mistakes, completely turning away from sin, and never going back to your old life. As Paul writes, "if anyone is in Christ, he is a new creation; old things have passed away; behold, all things have become new" (2 Corinthians 5:17). Repentance requires a complete change in your behavior and in your heart. If you answer Jesus' call to repentance, you will never be the same.

 IF anyone has ears to *hear,* let him HEAR.

MARK 4:23

If you are a parent, you know what selective listening is. A child often hears only what he or she wants to hear. The result is—at best—parental frustration, but depending on the words spoken, not hearing can be the beginning of a bad situation.

Selective listening is also an issue when it comes to hearing the gospel. Jesus called for all who will hear the gospel to heed its message. One day all that has been kept secret will come out into the light. With that warning in mind, you can choose not to hear about your sin and then foolishly continue in darkness. But when you choose to hear the gospel—when you decide to let go of your own ideas about life—then you hear God's loving call, a call you might have heard much earlier if you had "ears to hear."

The noisy world can make it hard for your ears to hear God's voice. The enemy can interfere and your self-reliance can make you deaf at times, but God will give you ears to hear His voice if you are willing to hear.

"PEACE, *be still!*"
And the wind ceased
and there was a great calm.

Mark 4:39

At the end of a day devoted to ministering in Capernaum, Jesus decided to take a boat with His disciples to travel to the other side of the Sea of Galilee. Weary, Jesus lay down to sleep. While He was asleep, a storm arose that panicked the disciples. The storm was strong enough to frighten even the fishermen on board the boat, men who knew water and waves and wind, but the storm was not severe enough to awaken Jesus.

Whether they wanted Jesus to be awake fully for their collective demise or they thought perhaps He could remedy the situation, the disciples woke up the Teacher. Jesus stood up, "rebuked the wind, and said to the sea, 'Peace, be still!'" Immediately, the wind ceased and calmness presided over the sea. As a result, the disciples' fear changed to awe at the mighty power of Jesus, whom even the wind and the sea obeyed. Jesus then chastised the disciples for their lack of faith.

The one who calmed the storm on the Sea of Galilee can also calm any internal storm you experience. Go to Him when the waves of anxiety and winds of uncertainty threaten to overwhelm. He will say, "Peace, be still!"

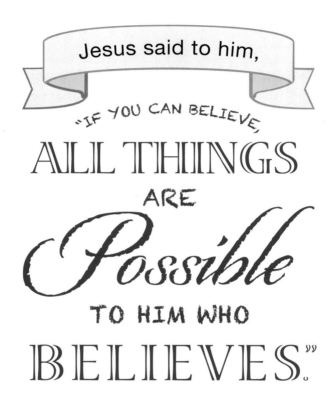

Jesus said to him,

"IF YOU CAN BELIEVE,

ALL THINGS

ARE

Possible

TO HIM WHO

BELIEVES."

MARK 9:23

If you wholeheartedly believe in the Lord, all things truly are possible. As the experience of the father in Mark 9 teaches, all things are still possible even when your faith is imperfect.

A man approached Jesus and asked for his son to be healed of an evil spirit. The man had asked Jesus' disciples to cast out the spirit, but they were unable to do so. Jesus asked for the boy to be brought to Him, at which time the boy convulsed and foamed at the mouth. In spite of this, Jesus stated, "All things are possible to him who believes." Immediately, Mark reports, the father cried out, "Lord, I believe; help my unbelief!" (v. 24), and then Jesus healed the boy.

The father's prayer can be your prayer and a lifeline when you're struggling. So can the truth that Jesus spoke: "All things are possible to him who believes." This denotes your faith when praying to God. The Bible clearly teaches you must approach God in faith to attain the requests presented to Him. This doesn't mean you will always receive what you want, but you can trust God's timing and perfect will, and know He will answer you.

WHOEVER

RECEIVES ME,

RECEIVES NOT ME BUT

HIM

WHO SENT ME.

MARK 9:37

On the way to Capernaum, Jesus heard the disciples arguing about which of them was the greatest. Jesus said: "If anyone desires to be first, he shall be last of all and servant of all" (v. 35). To drive the point home, Jesus continued, "Whoever receives one of these little children in My name receives Me" (v. 37). To be great in the kingdom of God, one must have a spirit of servitude.

Jesus wanted His disciples to serve everyone, even someone as lowly as a child (who was marginalized in the culture of His day). Jesus' words connoted a willingness to serve in unseen ways, to do work no one else wants to do, and to serve without drawing attention to oneself.

Finally, Jesus said the one who receives a child in Jesus' name receives not only Him but the Father also. God had sent His Son to earth to serve and give His life as the atonement for sin. In order to receive God's salvation, people need to accept His Son. This requires a humble heart willing to listen to Jesus' words.

A mark of your Christianity is your willingness to serve others. Ask God to give you a servant's heart so you can serve even the least in society.

MANY WHO ARE

FIRST

WILL BE LAST,

AND

THE **LAST**

FIRST.

— MARK 10:31 —

Today's passage follows Jesus' encounter with the rich young ruler. Jesus told the young man he needed to sell his goods and give the money to the poor in order to gain eternal life. After the young man left, Jesus told His disciples those who follow Him must be willing to abandon all for His sake.

The way God wants you to live is different from the world's ways. Fulfilling God's call to serve humbly does not put you in the world's spotlight. You will find yourself with the unnoticed—with the widow and orphan, the poverty-stricken and homeless, the sick and the imprisoned. The world prefers people who are setting sports records, producing movies, or making lots of money. They may be first in the world's eyes, but—depending on their hearts—last in God's kingdom.

At the same time, those faithful followers of Jesus who are visiting people in prison, sitting at the bedside of the elderly and forgotten, serving in soup kitchens, helping underprivileged children—these are the first in God's kingdom. They have chosen to serve people in obedience to their Lord and for His glory.

WHENEVER YOU STAND

praying,

IF YOU HAVE ANYTHING

AGAINST ANYONE,

FORGIVE

HIM.

MARK 11:25

Jesus told His disciples if they wanted direct access to God through prayer, then they needed to forgive those who had hurt them. If they would not forgive others, then how could they expect God to forgive them?

God's commands are always for people's good, and here is His command to forgive others. That sounds simple enough, but depending on the harm done, who did the harming, and the aftermath of that incident, the act of forgiving can be extremely difficult.

However, the act of forgiving can also be extremely freeing. When you forgive others, you lay down your heavy burdens of resentment, anger, and fractured relationships. The act of forgiving also removes a barrier between you and God, and your forgiving others enables you to receive the forgiveness you need from Him.

You live in a broken world that is populated by fellow sinners. Thus, you will experience offenses and hurts that you'll need to forgive—and you will offend and hurt others. God wants you to have access to Him in prayer, and forgiving those who have wronged you is the key.

You shall

Love

your neighbor
as yourself.

MARK 12:31

Have you ever been asked about your Christian beliefs only to realize that the person just wanted to start an argument? In contrast, perhaps you've had theological discussions with those who truly were curious about the Bible.

In Mark 12 some Sadducees approached Jesus with the same hostility and closed-mindedness you might have encountered from the former person. But a scribe who truly wanted to know the answer later approached Jesus: "Which is the first commandment of all?" (v. 28).

In response, Jesus gave the first two commandments of all: to love God with all your heart, soul, mind, strength; and to treat your neighbors in the kind and loving way you want them to treat you. The scribe concluded Jesus was correct, and Jesus said this scribe was "not far from the kingdom of God" (v. 34).

When you show love to others, you are following the second command and living your obedience to the first. While loving others may not always be easy, the Holy Spirit can guide you in showing the love of Jesus in your daily actions and words.

FOR THEY ALL
PUT IN OUT OF THEIR
ABUNDANCE,
BUT SHE OUT OF HER

poverty

PUT IN ALL
THAT SHE HAD,
HER WHOLE LIVELIHOOD.

MARK 12:44

Jesus and His disciples were at the temple and could see people give their monetary offerings to their Lord. They saw many rich people make a show of the amount of money they contributed, but then they saw a poor widow give only two mites for her offering. Yet instead of praising the ones who had given an excessive amount to the temple, Jesus praised the lowly widow.

Aren't we blessed that Jesus looks at our hearts, not our bank accounts, when we give our offerings? We are also blessed that He looks at our sacrifice, not just at the amount we are giving to Him. If He looked only at the amount, Jesus would not have commended the widow in Mark 12 for putting only two mites into the treasury.

The widow's two mites were far more valuable to Jesus than the gifts of the rich people. The widow had given all she had and made a true sacrifice. In your own giving of tithes and offerings, emulate the example of the widow and give sacrificially from the heart.

He who
ENDURES
to the end
shall be **SAVED.**

MARK 13:13

Today's passage comes from Mark's account of the Olivet Discourse, where Jesus prophesied that His disciples would face severe persecution for following Him. As a result, a clear line of division would be made between Jesus' disciples and the world.

Jesus even experienced this division within His own earthly family (John 7:5), and He told His early disciples, "I have come to 'set a man against his father, a daughter against her mother' . . . and 'a man's enemies will be those of his own household'" (Matthew 10:35–36).

This kind of division, Jesus taught, has become more pronounced as the end times approach. "Brother will betray brother to death, and a father his child; and children will rise up against parents and cause them to be put to death" (Mark 13:12). Christians all around the world would face persecution from their families. In addition, they "will be hated by all" (v. 13) simply because they follow Jesus.

Enduring persecution for your faith will never be easy, but the Holy Spirit will strengthen and guide you. Jesus promises if you are faithful to Him and stand firm in your love for Him, you will be saved.

But of that day
and hour
[when Jesus returns]
no one knows,
not even the angels in heaven,
nor the Son, but only the Father.

MARK 13:32

Today's verse continues Jesus' Olivet Discourse. According to Jesus, in the last days there would be earthquakes, famine, false teachers, "wars and rumors of wars," and "nation will rise against nation" (vv. 7, 8). Followers of Jesus would be arrested, beaten, and forced to defend their faith before synagogue councils as well as rulers and kings.

Then Jesus shared some details about His return: "The sun will be darkened, and the moon will not give its light; the stars of heaven will fall, and the powers in the heavens will be shaken. Then they will see the Son of Man coming in the clouds with great power and glory" (vv. 24–26). These events will precede Jesus' coming back to set up His eternal kingdom on earth. But Jesus didn't state when He will return. As today's verse shows, not even Jesus knows the date of His return.

May not knowing when Jesus will return keep you vigilant and alert as it fuels your efforts to share the news of Jesus' love with those who haven't heard the gospel. Also, may the news of His return encourage you when you are forced to defend your faith.

Take, eat; this is
MY BODY....

This is **MY BLOOD**
of the new covenant,
which is shed for many.

MARK 14:22, 24

"This is My body. . . . This is My blood." These words are at the heart of the Lord's Supper. When you partake of the bread and the wine, you remember the broken and bleeding body of Jesus, broken for you when He absorbed the holy God's wrath on the cross.

When Jesus ate with His disciples in the upper room, He picked up a cup of wine and said, "This is My blood," anticipating the blood He would shed on the cross, blood that hearkened back to the first Passover in Egypt as well as the animal sacrifices for sin made throughout Israel's history. When Jesus would die on Calvary, the perfect Lamb of God would be slain, the necessary sacrifice for humanity's sins. This sacrifice would provide the way for men and women to reconcile with God.

Because of Jesus' sacrifice, you can approach God's throne and thank Him for sending His Son to die for your sins, ask forgiveness for your sins, praise your heavenly Father, place petitions before Him, and ask Him to guide you through life until you are home with Him for eternity.

NEVERTHELESS,

NOT WHAT I WILL,

BUT WHAT

YOU

WILL.

MARK 14:36

Because you are human, times will arise that will test your faith in God. A tragedy might occur that causes you to question His will, or the pace at which He answers your prayers might frustrate you. When you face such situations in life, you must learn to trust God's will and believe He will work the situations for your overall good.

That was the very situation Jesus faced in the Garden of Gethsemane after He and His disciples left the upper room. Jesus knew the cross was imminent. The time was near when He would give His life for the sins of the world. While praying, Jesus told His Father that He did not want to die on the cross, yet He willingly submitted Himself to the Father's will and yielded to it—even to the point of death. This submission by the Son to the Father speaks of the great love Jesus had for His Father.

Should you ever encounter such a situation that tests your commitment to God, may you rely on the strength of the Holy Spirit to help you yield to God's good and perfect will, which is sometimes unfathomable and mysterious.

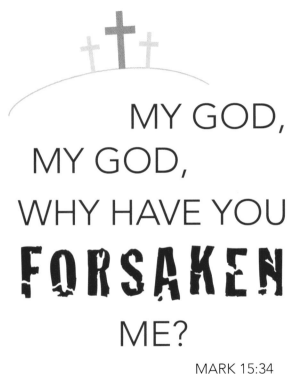

MY GOD,
MY GOD,
WHY HAVE YOU
FORSAKEN
ME?

MARK 15:34

The time came for Jesus to drink of the cup He had prayed to be taken from Him in the Garden of Gethsemane. Shortly after finishing His prayer, Roman soldiers arrested Jesus and tried Him before Pontius Pilate. To appease the crowds, Pilate condemned Jesus to death, even though Pilate had found no sin in Him. Eventually, the soldiers led Jesus to Calvary and placed Him on the cross. In His darkest hour, with the sins of the whole world—of every person throughout all time—on His back, Jesus cried out, "My God, My God, why have You forsaken Me?"

How haunting—even chilling—are those words. Maybe you have felt forsaken by God at some point. God did allow His only Son to suffer an undeserved punishment on your behalf. But God did not forsake His Son; He raised Him from the dead. Because of Jesus' sacrifice and God's great power, you have been given the gift of eternal life.

May you live a life of gratitude, humbled by this love. May you be ready for God to use you to share with others the good news of His life-changing love.

THE SPIRIT

of the

LORD

is upon

ME.

Luke 4:18

The saying "you can't go home again" reflects the experience of many people, including Jesus. Having begun His Galilean ministry, Jesus went to the synagogue in His hometown of Nazareth, as was His practice. Someone handed Him a scroll containing the words of Isaiah, and He read a passage from Isaiah that the Jews would recognize as describing the Messiah. Jesus concluded with, "Today this Scripture is fulfilled in your hearing" (Luke 4:21), leaving no doubt about His claim to be the Messiah.

Initially some people marveled at His teaching, but Jesus' hometown did not accept Him. An angry mob drove Him from the synagogue and out of town. Those citizens of Nazareth could not accept that the local carpenter's son was the long-awaited Messiah.

Jesus wanted to minister to the people of His hometown, and He wants to bring lost people into His kingdom today. When you share the gospel with others, you also might be rejected by those who know you well. When such times arise, remember Jesus also faced rejection but didn't let that deter Him.

I HAVE NOT COME TO CALL THE

RIGHTEOUS,

but

to

REPENTANCE.

LUKE 5:32

Feeling that their prestigious positions and power were being threatened, the scribes and Pharisees continually questioned the words and actions of Jesus. They questioned, for instance, why He ate with tax collectors and sinners after Jesus had dined with Levi, a tax collector. The scribes and Pharisees never would have openly socialized with the lowest in society. Jesus responded with a straightforward comment: it's the people who are sick who need to be made well (v. 31).

Jesus applied that medical principle to the spiritual health of men and women. People who were aware of their sinfulness were the ones who would hear Jesus' message of repentance, forgiveness, and freedom from sin. On the other hand, the law-keeping and judgmental scribes and Pharisees, who were just as spiritually sick and sinful, did not—or would not—recognize it.

May you not be judgmental like the scribes and Pharisees when you see people whose walk with Jesus and whose worship of Him are different from yours. And may you strive not to be blind to the lowest in society who need to know the healing message of repentance and forgiveness.

Blessed

are you

when men

hate you . . .

for the

Son of Man's

sake.

Luke 6:22

The Beatitudes offer encouragement and a biblical perspective for people who are suffering and downtrodden. Consider today's verse with its rather jarring and puzzling start. At first glance, you might find it hard to feel blessed—to feel all is well in your soul and in your relationship with God—when people hate you because of your commitment to the cause of Christ. Yet this is what Jesus promised in this beatitude.

When people persecute you because of your commitment to Him, remember you are in good company. Jesus experienced rejection and hatred, and New Testament heroes such as Stephen, Peter, and Paul faced persecution, even to the point of death. Since the early days of the church, thousands of Christians have faced persecution and martyrdom for the sake of the gospel. You are not alone in your suffering.

But this beatitude from Luke ends with a promise: "Your reward is great in heaven" (v. 23). May you hold on to this truth when you experience persecution for your faith, being mindful the Lord is with you and you will one day experience eternity with Him.

JUDGE NOT,

 and you shall not be judged.

CONDEMN NOT,

 and you shall not be condemned.

FORGIVE,

and you will be forgiven."

Luke 6:37

Jesus' Sermon on the Plain contained teachings on how Christians should live. For example, in Luke 6:37–38, Jesus gave four specific commands: "Judge not, and you shall not be judged. Condemn not, and you shall not be condemned. Forgive, and you will be forgiven. Give, and it will be given to you." All of these address how Christians should treat others and how they are to honor God with their time, talents, and treasures. Jesus said the same measure in which we follow these commands will be used to measure against us.

When you judge others, you show pride, coming to harsh conclusions about people, perhaps based on very little truth. When you condemn others, you take that harshness further, perhaps going public with your criticism. When you hold a grudge, you close the door to God's forgiveness of yourself. When you selfishly hold on to your time, talents, and resources rather than supporting the work of the Lord, you fail to be a good steward of God's blessings. Thus, shine God's light by not judging and condemning others. Shine His light by forgiving others and giving of your time, talents, and resources.

A good tree does not bear **BAD FRUIT,** nor does a **BAD TREE** bear *good fruit.*

Luke 6:43

Jesus continued His Sermon on the Plain by discussing the fruit that identifies Christians. One doesn't need to know a lot of specifics such as the shape of its leaves, the texture of its bark, or its general height to determine a tree's type. A tree is known by its fruit, and as today's verse says, "A good tree does not bear bad fruit."

The fruits to which Jesus referred are the words and actions of a Christian. The fruit of the Spirit, as listed in Galatians 5:22–23, should be evident in a Christian's everyday life.

Like the trees Jesus spoke of here, you are known by the fruit you bear. If you are strong in the Lord—if you are a good tree—you will not bear bad fruit. What kind of fruit do you bear? Do you show love, kindness, patience, and self-control to your coworkers, family, and friends?

If you want to honor the Lord, reach out to people, love them with His love, and serve with humility and grace. Your words and actions of love will indeed be good fruit.

I say to you,

I HAVE NOT
	FOUND SUCH GREAT

Faith,

NOT EVEN IN ISRAEL!

LUKE 7:9

A Roman centurion's representatives told Jesus that the centurion's servant was sick and on the verge of death. Without hesitation, Jesus followed the representatives back to the centurion's home.

Before Jesus arrived at the house, the centurion's friends met Him with a message. The centurion acknowledged Jesus didn't need to go to his home for the healing to happen. Rather, all Jesus needed to do was "say the word, and my servant will be healed" (Luke 7:7). Jesus marveled at this statement of faith and commended the centurion: "I have not found such great faith, not even in Israel!" Quite remarkably, this was a Roman pagan who had placed such great faith in Jesus. Those who returned back to the home found the servant had been healed.

Even today you might hear of people whose faith in God seems much stronger than yours. Rather than comparing yourself to them, instead be encouraged by their faith. May you be inspired by their example—and may you be mindful that God responds even to faith the size of a mustard seed (Matthew 17:20).

FOR WHAT PROFIT
IS IT TO A MAN
IF HE GAINS THE WHOLE

WORLD,

 IS HIMSELF
DESTROYED OR
LOST?

LUKE 9:25

In Luke 9:23–27, Jesus warned His disciples of the great cost of following Him. If one wants to be a disciple, then he or she must take up a cross and follow Jesus. Those who deny themselves for the sake of the gospel will experience true spiritual fulfillment and eternal life with God. Conversely, those who devote themselves to gaining the riches of the world might gain everything on earth but will lose everything eternally, including their souls.

Gaining the whole world may sound quite appealing, but everyone ultimately faces the question: What is such an endeavor really worth? Focusing on life in this present world can come at the cost of a person's soul.

All that the world offers is temporary. Tragically, the world makes it much too easy to push aside the time you could be investing in something much more valuable: your eternal relationship with God. Keep your perspective in the right place about the material possessions of the world and continue to take up your cross in following Jesus. If you will deny yourself in this life, you will gain the riches of eternal life with Him.

BUT THE VERY
HAIRS OF YOUR HEAD
ARE ALL NUMBERED.
DO NOT
FEAR THEREFORE;
YOU ARE OF MORE VALUE
THAN MANY SPARROWS.

LUKE 12:7

In Luke 12:4–7, Jesus told His followers not to fear those who can harm them because God is ultimately in control. God cares greatly about His followers when they experience pain and suffering. This stems from the watchful care God has for all of His creation. The Almighty who keeps the planets in their orbits is at the same time aware of a lowly sparrow that falls to the ground. Since He is even aware of what most would consider an insignificant event, how much more is He aware of the concerns of His children?

As Jesus said, "You are of more value than many sparrows." Jesus pointed out that "five sparrows [are] sold for two copper coins" (v. 6). As for your value, Jesus died on the cross to save you from sin and eternal separation from God. Having died for you, Jesus commits Himself to caring for you. He cares so much for you He even knows how many hairs are on your head.

When you name Jesus as your Savior and honor Him with your life, you need not fear anything in this world. You can rest knowing God's caring eye is watching over you.

FOR WHOEVER EXALTS HIM SELF WILL BE *humbled,* AND HE WHO HUMBLES HIMSELF WILL BE *Exalted.*

LUKE 14:11

On a particular Sabbath Jesus went to the house of a Pharisee to eat. While dining, Jesus noticed guests vying to sit at the places of honor at the table. Jesus offered counsel to these individuals: "When you are invited . . . to a wedding feast, do not sit down in the best place, lest one more honorable than you be invited by him; and he who invited you and him come and say to you, 'Give place to this man,' and then you begin with shame to take the lowest place" (vv. 8–9). To be removed publically from a place of honor would be more humiliating than having sat in the lowest place.

Jesus continued: "But when you are invited, go and sit down in the lowest place, so that when he who invited you comes he may say to you, 'Friend, go up higher'" (v. 10). With this counsel, Jesus illustrated what He wanted to teach: "Whoever exalts himself will be humbled, and he who humbles himself will be exalted."

You are to serve God and love your neighbors from a place of humility. If you do this, God will exalt you in His perfect timing.

There is joy

IN THE PRESENCE OF

THE angels of God

over ONE

sinner WHO REPENTS.

LUKE 15:10

You've undoubtedly had the experience of misplacing something and then searching for it. Perhaps you even looked in places where you knew it absolutely couldn't be, so desperate you were to find it. And when you found it, how did you respond? Did you feel so overjoyed that you had to share the news?

This passage in Luke describes the joy of a woman after she found something she had lost. In Jesus' parable, a woman lost a silver coin, and then swept the house looking for it. When she finally found the lost coin, she called together her friends and neighbors: "Rejoice with me, for I have found the piece which I lost!" (v. 9). Her joy was unmistakable.

For this woman, her coin represented a significant loss, and the joy she felt was genuine and worth sharing. Jesus then compared this joy with the joy in heaven "over one sinner who repents." Imagine the heartfelt joy of the angels when they rejoice over a sinner who has received salvation. Now imagine the joy and celebration that heaven experienced on the day you repented.

HE WHO

IS *faithful*

IN WHAT IS

least

IS *faithful* ALSO

IN **MUCH.**

LUKE 16:10

In Luke 16, Jesus told a parable about a dishonest steward or manager who mishandled his master's business. When the master asked him for an accounting and said he would be released from his position, the steward came up with a shrewd plan to ingratiate himself with his master's debtors so they would treat him well when he was no longer employed. The steward reduced the amount each one owed, cheating the master while gaining favor with other businessmen. The master praised the steward's shrewdness, but Jesus pointed out that anyone who created relationships through unrighteous means would not be trusted with righteous things of great value in God's kingdom.

You may be successful, making shrewd deals and influencing people for personal gain, but that will not necessarily impress God. God wants you to use your talents and finances to further His kingdom whether it results in your personal gain or not. When you use your gifts to spread the gospel, creating relationships for eternity, God will trust you with more opportunities and greater responsibilities in the advancement of His kingdom. May you be faithful with God's trust.

IF YOUR BROTHER
. . . REPENTS,

FORGIVE

LUKE 17:3

HIM.

Forgiveness or its absence can make a huge difference in our relationships with others. When we carry a grudge, we weigh ourselves down. When we refuse to forgive someone who has offended us, we build a wall that needs to be torn down. Forgiveness is the only option to rid ourselves of such burdensome grudges.

Jesus talked about the importance of forgiving others. He also set no limits on how much His disciples should forgive individuals who continue to offend them. Jesus said even if someone sins against one of His disciples seven times in one day, then this person should still receive forgiveness every time.

Think about the many times Jesus has forgiven you when you have sinned. In turn, He expects you to forgive others just as you have been forgiven. If you want to be forgiven by God for your sins, then you must be willing to forgive those who have sinned against you.

When you choose to forgive someone, you replace anger and resentment with peace and love. Forgiveness is a blessing to both the one being forgiven and the one showing forgiveness.

My
house is
A HOUSE
of PRAYER.

LUKE 19:46

During Jesus' time the temple was the central location for the Jews to worship God. Unfortunately, not everyone respected the sacredness of the temple, and many often used the temple grounds as a place to make a profit. In addition, some unscrupulous business practices could also be found. If a family brought an animal to sacrifice, a crooked official could find a blemish, forcing the family to purchase a different animal.

Because the temple was holy and it was His Father's house of worship, this behavior infuriated Jesus. As a result, Jesus chased the merchants out of the temple, crying out, "'My house is a house of prayer,' but you have made it a 'den of thieves'" (v. 46), which were first recorded in Isaiah 56:7 and Jeremiah 7:11. Jesus refused to allow these people to desecrate His Father's house.

The temple is no longer standing today, but God's presence now dwells within all of His people through the Holy Spirit. Even so, church buildings today, whether elaborate or modest, are still houses for prayer as well as sacred places to worship your heavenly Father. Remember to honor God's house as a place of worship when you enter its doors.

RENDER *therefore* TO CAESAR THE THINGS THAT ARE CAESAR'S, *and* TO GOD THE THINGS THAT ARE GOD'S.

LUKE 20:25

The Jewish religious leaders weren't subtle in their attempts to force Jesus to say something that would get Him in trouble with the Roman authorities. In this instance, they raised the issue of paying taxes to Caesar. Jesus asked them: "Whose image and inscription does [a denarius] have?" (Luke 20:24). When they acknowledged Caesar's likeness was on a denarius, Jesus responded, "Render therefore to Caesar the things that are Caesar's, and to God the things that are God's." God had ultimately placed the Romans in charge of the Jews, and they owed their respect and services to this governing authority.

Christians are to obey the authorities that their sovereign God has allowed to come into power—unless they require something that conflicts with God's law. In those situations, they should render their obedience to God first, for He is the ultimate authority.

You owe your allegiance to your country. Seek to uphold the law. God has ordained the leaders that lead the country, and you should pray for your leaders to govern the country in a way that honors God.

HEAVEN AND EARTH WILL PASS AWAY, BUT MY WORDS WILL BY NO MEANS PASS AWAY.

LUKE 21:33

Luke 21 contains Luke's account of Jesus speaking to His disciples about the end times. Jesus called them—and He called us—to watch for the signs He has outlined. Jesus spoke of wars, calamities, and destruction that will be prevalent. Those signs will indicate the time is near when "heaven and earth will pass away."

Jesus realized His disciples' reactions to these teachings would range from unsettledness to sheer terror, so Jesus concluded with words of hope. The created world will pass away, but Jesus' words—His eternal truths—will "by no means pass away." With this promise, Jesus echoed the prophet Isaiah who had preached: "The grass withers, the flower fades, but the word of our God stands forever" (40:8). Though this world will fade away, the words of Jesus will endure forever.

You know from God's Word that Satan—and sin and death—will ultimately be defeated and Jesus will reign forever. God's Word, His kingdom, His love, and His rule will be eternal. As you look for the signs of the last days, take comfort in knowing these truths.

PETER,

THE ROOSTER
SHALL NOT CROW
THIS DAY
BEFORE YOU WILL DENY
THREE TIMES
THAT YOU KNOW ME.

Luke 22:34

Shortly after He had instituted the Lord's Supper, Jesus told Peter that Satan had asked if he "could sift [Peter] as wheat" (v. 31). Peter responded by proudly proclaiming he was willing to go both to prison and the grave for His Lord. Jesus then prophesied Peter would deny Him three times before the dawn of the next day. One can only imagine the embarrassment and indignation Peter felt when he heard these words. After he had followed Jesus for three years, why did Jesus say Peter would abandon Him?

Many times, you may be like Peter—much too confident in your abilities to stand for Jesus and for what you believe. Yet when the pressure comes, you sometimes fail, just like Peter, leaving you disappointed in yourself because you have let down your Lord. Trying to stand up for your faith in your own strength rather than calling on God to help is a dangerous proposition.

Satan may be working behind the scenes to set you up for spiritual failure, and you make his job too easy when you count on mere human strength and willpower to keep you faithful. When you find yourself needing to take a stand for Jesus, call on Him to help you.

FATHER,
IF IT IS
Y OUR
will,
TAKE THIS
CUP
away
FROM ME.

Luke 22:42

Soon after prophesying Peter's denial, Jesus found Himself alone praying to His Father. The anguish in Jesus' words is unmistakable—and perfectly understandable. As He knelt in the Garden of Gethsemane, He knew what lay ahead. He knew of Judas' upcoming betrayal, the unfair trial, the conviction despite His innocence, the mocking, the crucifixion—and the separation from His Father when He paid the price for sin.

"Father, if it is Your will, take this cup away from Me." Praying so fervently and with such passion that "His sweat became like great drops of blood" (v. 44), Jesus nevertheless submitted to the will of His Father. Jesus did not want to suffer what was coming, but He was sinless and obedient, and He accepted the excruciatingly painful death on the cross.

By God's grace, may you never face similar agonizing pain—physical, emotional, and spiritual—such as Jesus experienced in the hours between praying in the garden and being crucified. But if you must take of the cup of suffering, you can be confident God will be with you in your hour of need.

Today
YOU WILL
BE WITH
Me
IN
Paradise.

Luke 23:43

After Pilate sentenced Jesus to death, the Roman soldiers led Jesus to Golgotha and placed Him on a cross between two criminals. One of the men mocked Jesus: "If You are the Christ, save Yourself and us!" (v. 39). In sharp contrast came the words of the other criminal: "Lord, remember me when You come into Your kingdom" (v. 42). Jesus heard this broken man's request and accepted it as a genuine expression of faith. "Today you will be with Me in Paradise," Jesus promised.

Did this criminal deserve mercy? No—but no one does. All of humanity is sinful and in need of God's forgiveness and mercy. Whether one has been convicted of a crime while another one has just told a lie, both are equally sinful in God's eyes. But both can also receive forgiveness and the salvation that comes from putting one's faith in Jesus.

God's grace saved you when you recognized your sinfulness and the forgiveness you could receive because of Jesus' death on the cross. Salvation is not based on your merit but is entirely a gift from God. Furthermore, just like the criminal on the cross, you have the promise of one day being with Jesus in heaven.

BEHOLD

My hands

AND

My feet,

THAT IT IS I

MYSELF.

LUKE 24:39

Throughout His ministry Jesus had been open about His forthcoming resurrection. He had talked about spending three days and nights in the heart of the earth just as Jonah had been in the belly of the fish and about rebuilding the temple in three days. He had even explicitly told them He would rise again.

The fact remained, though, the disciples didn't fully expect to see the resurrected Jesus—and when He appeared among them, they were terrified. They thought they had seen a spirit, but Jesus showed them His hands and feet and said, "Handle Me and see, for a spirit does not have flesh and bones as you see I have" (Luke 24:39). Jesus wanted to demonstrate He was there in the flesh. The resurrection proved Jesus' power over sin and death, and fulfilled Jesus' own prophecies.

Jesus' resurrection also gave the disciples the fortitude to stand for their risen Lord—whom they had seen with their own eyes and felt with their own hands—even to the point of death. Their testimonies can help strengthen your faith in your Lord and King.

FOR GOD

SO *Loved*

THE WORLD THAT

HE GAVE HIS ONLY BEGOTTEN

SON, THAT WHOEVER

BELIEVES IN HIM

SHOULD

not perish

BUT HAVE

EVERLASTING LIFE.

JOHN 3:16

Good teachers know how to ask good questions that will get their students to think. But in his conversation with Jesus, the esteemed teacher Nicodemus asked good questions for his own edification and eventual salvation.

Nicodemus came by night and asked Jesus what he must do to gain salvation. Jesus explained one must be born again to be saved. This confused Nicodemus because he thought he would have to be born again physically from his mother's womb, but Jesus explained to Nicodemus that he needed a spiritual rebirth. This spiritual rebirth would occur when Nicodemus placed his total faith in Jesus, God's own Son, who had been sent to save the world from sin.

Nicodemus asked the right questions and learned how to be born again. Those who place their faith in Jesus will never be condemned because of His sacrificial death on the cross. Instead, they "should not perish but have everlasting life." Have you experienced this spiritual rebirth?

Whoever DRINKS OF THE water THAT I SHALL GIVE HIM WILL NEVER thirst.

JOHN 4:14

The Jews had intense hatred for the Samaritans because they were descended from Jews who had married Gentiles. But when Jesus traveled through Samaria in John 4, He exhibited a different mindset.

When Jesus stopped at a well, a Samaritan woman approached, and Jesus asked her for a drink of water. Jesus knew His physical thirst was not as important as her spiritual thirst. Jesus promised to quench the woman's spiritual thirst with living water that would make her never thirst again. This stunned the woman, and she asked for the water He offered.

Jesus asked the woman to fetch her husband, but the woman claimed to be unmarried. Jesus acknowledged the woman didn't have a husband because she had been married five times. For the woman, Jesus' knowledge of her personal life proved Him to be a prophet (and later that He was the foretold Messiah).

Jesus still offers people living water today. Drinking of this water means never thirsting spiritually again. Have you quenched your spiritual thirst? If so, ask God to show you those thirsty for living water.

God is Spirit,

and those who worship Him

MUST worship in

spirit & truth.

John 4:24

Today's verse comes from Jesus' discussion with the Samaritan woman. After she had recognized Jesus was a prophet, the woman pointed out that the Jews worshiped in Jerusalem whereas the Samaritans had their own temple on Mount Gerizim where they worshiped because of their mixed heritage. Thus, the Samaritans didn't have the same direct access to worship God.

Jesus told the woman the hour was soon coming when people could worship the Father anywhere as long as they worshiped Him "in spirit and truth." God would not care about a person's heritage as long as the person truly loved and worshiped Him. All would have equal access to the Father.

Jesus knows your heart. Therefore, He knows the heart you bring to a time of worship. He knows your motives for going to worship—be it out of a sense of duty or joy. He knows how focused you are on the singing and the message from the pulpit. God wants you to worship Him with a heart fully devoted to Him.

Before you enter church this weekend, ask God to give you an open and expectant heart. Strive to worship Him fully in spirit and in truth.

MOST ASSUREDLY, I SAY TO YOU,

HE WHO HEARS

MY WORD AND BELIEVES

IN HIM WHO SENT ME

HAS EVERLASTING LIFE.

JOHN 5:24

Throughout His ministry, Jesus made it clear that He was the only way to heaven. John 5:24–30 offers a clear picture of what happens to men and women after they die. All will give an account, and how one viewed God's Son while on earth will have eternal consequences.

Those who accept Jesus will experience eternity in heaven with God, and those who reject Him will suffer eternity in hell separated from God. These are the only two options. No middle ground exists on which to stand. This reality is not politically correct in a postmodern age where almost every action and belief is tolerated. Morality is gray as opposed to a well-defined standard of good and evil.

Despite the way today's culture defines life after death, the truth of Jesus' words remains: every person will one day stand before God at the judgment, and every person's eternal destiny will be pronounced. Everyone who walks with God on this earth will have eternal life with Him. Those who reject Jesus' claim to be God's Son will spend eternity apart from God. Eternity is a long time. What choice have you made? And what about those you love?

THE VERY WORKS THAT I DO—

BEAR WITNESS OF ME,

THAT THE

Father

HAS SENT ME.

JOHN 5:36

The identity of Jesus has been the source of discussions for two thousand years. You cannot simply say Jesus was a good moral teacher because in addition to teaching moral principles He also claimed to be God. This means He either really is God, or He is a masterful liar seeking fame, or an insane person confused about His identity. You must decide which of the three conclusions describes Jesus.

Time and time again, Jesus made it clear He was the Son of God. For example, in today's verse, Jesus asserted the Father had sent Him to earth. In addition to this, both John the Baptist and the Father had testified He was God's Son: "When He had been baptized, Jesus came up immediately from the water; and behold, the heavens were opened to Him, and He saw the Spirit of God descending like a dove and alighting upon Him. And suddenly a voice came from heaven, saying, 'This is My beloved Son, in whom I am well pleased'" (Matthew 3:16–17). Events such as these showed Jesus truly is the Son of God.

You will gain life everlasting only if you repent, accept Jesus' identity as God's Son, and ask Him to be your Lord. What is your conclusion about the true identity of Jesus?

I AM

THE

bread of life.

HE WHO	HE WHO
COMES TO	BELIEVES IN
Me	*Me*
SHALL NEVER	SHALL NEVER
HUNGER, AND	**THIRST.**

JOHN 6:35

In the Gospel of John, Jesus made powerful declarations of His equality with God. Each of these statements started with "I am" and to the Jews clearly echoed God's identifying Himself to Moses as "I AM WHO I AM" (Exodus 3:14).

Jesus' first "I am" statement was "I am the bread of life." This also relates to the discussion between Jesus and the people about God's sending manna from heaven. After identifying Himself as the Bread of Life, Jesus continued: "Your fathers ate the manna in the wilderness, and are dead. This is the bread which comes down from heaven, that one may eat of it and not die" (John 6:49–50). Those who ate of the bread being offered now would gain eternal life as opposed to the temporary physical satisfaction experienced in the wilderness.

Jesus came down from heaven in God's perfect timing. But unlike manna that only preserves physical life, Jesus—the Bread of Life—preserves spiritual life for eternity. He alone can satisfy your hungering soul while you live on this earth in preparation for eternity.

IF ANYONE THIRSTS, LET HIM

come to Me

AND DRINK.

JOHN 7:37

Because God created you to have a relationship with Him, your deepest needs cannot be met except by Him. Only Jesus can satisfy your spiritual thirst. Those who drink from Him will have "rivers of living water" flowing from their hearts (v. 38). People, though, can spend their lives trying to satisfy an inner sense of unsettledness. Maybe they search for a better job, a bigger home, or a better relationship. Yet the material possessions of this world can only satisfy for a short time.

French mathematician and author Blaise Pascal described both the problem and the solution to this dilemma: "There is a God-shaped vacuum in the heart of every man which cannot be filled by any created thing, but only by God, the Creator, made known through Jesus." Pascal asserted the natural void that exists in everyone can only be filled by God.

Consider the thirst with which you are all too familiar. Think about how you have tried to find satisfaction with the things of this world. Then accept Jesus' invitation: "Come to Me and drink." He waits to fill the "God-shaped vacuum" in your heart.

I AM
THE LIGHT
OF
THE WORLD.
HE WHO
FOLLOWS ME
SHALL NOT
WALK IN
DARKNESS.

JOHN 8:12

John 8 opens with Jesus addressing a crowd of people when scribes and Pharisees bring Him a woman caught in adultery. They wanted to test Jesus, trying to trick Him into saying something contradictory to the Law of Moses. They asserted the Law of Moses taught that the woman should be stoned and wanted to know what Jesus thought.

Jesus had no trouble avoiding the trap. He simply stated: "He who is without sin among you, let him throw a stone at her first" (v. 7). Thus, the gracious and merciful Jesus leveled the playing field with that statement. Every one of the woman's accusers turned and walked away. Jesus then told the woman since no one was left to condemn her, neither did He. She was to go forth and sin no more. Jesus proclaimed He was the Light of the World and those who follow Him would not walk in darkness.

As the Light of the world, Jesus shines light onto the darkness of sin, encouraging you to turn away from it and toward Him. Because He is the Light of the World, He also offers you healing, truth, hope, and love. No reason remains for you to be in darkness anymore.

163

The

TRUTH

SHALL MAKE YOU

Free

JOHN 8:32

Seeking absolute truth is a fading value in our culture. Good and evil are increasingly becoming relative terms, resulting in people doing what is right in their own eyes, with no regard for the consequences of their actions. A lack of truth and integrity is wreaking havoc in society and creating bondage to sin.

To a world in spiritual bondage, Jesus said, "If you abide in My word, you are My disciples indeed. And you shall know the truth, and the truth shall make you free" (vv. 31–32). Even though the world may deny absolute truth today, Christians know the Word of God is a sure foundation of truth. Those who want to please God and live according to His standards know they must abide by the truth of the Scriptures. If they will follow His truth, they will be set free from the bondage of sin.

Are you abiding in God's Word—both studying and living what you learn? God's Word is His love letter to you. By walking in His truth, according to His guidelines, and in obedience to His commands, you will know the fulfilling life of spiritual freedom He has designed for you.

I AM THE DOOR.

IF anyone enters

BY ME,

HE WILL BE **SAVED.**

JOHN 10:9

John 10 contains another one of Jesus' "I am" statements. In today's verse, Jesus is the door to salvation. Jesus paints the picture of sheep that need to return to the fold to find protection. Those who want to be safe and have an abundant life can only find it by entering the door that He opens.

Jesus is not one of many doors to the Father; He is the only door. Jesus never spoke of Himself as one route among several paths to God. Rather, Jesus consistently claimed He is the only way for a sinful human being to enter into a relationship with a holy God. This declaration upsets advocates of other religions, and it angers the spokespeople for rampant twenty-first-century tolerance. Regardless of who this truth upsets, Jesus remains the only door to salvation.

Humanity is sinful, and only forgiven people cleansed of their sin can be in the presence of God. Jesus is the only one who can provide you an opening for a relationship with the Father. Proponents of other religions and philosophies are knocking on the wrong doors. Which door will you open?

I AM
THE GOOD
SHEPHERD;
& I KNOW
MY SHEEP.

JOHN 10:14

Today's verse builds upon the "I am" statement from the previous devotion. This time Jesus says He is the Good Shepherd who protects His sheep, even going so far as to give His life for them. Being a shepherd is a difficult task and not an occupation well respected by society. A shepherd is on duty constantly to offer protection from lurking predators and threatening diseases. Adding to the challenge, sheep are not smart—a flock will follow one sheep that starts moving—even off a cliff. Sheep definitely need a good shepherd to protect them.

In actuality, people are not much different from sheep. They often make unwise decisions, and they cannot defend themselves against their primary enemy, Satan. People, too, will follow the crowd in making poor choices. Thus, they also need a shepherd to guide them and protect them.

Jesus declares He is your Good Shepherd and you are His sheep. As your Good Shepherd, He demonstrated His love already by giving His life for you on the cross.

Further, He cares for you as you submit to His guidance and He protects you from temptation and evil.

MY SHEEP
HEAR MY VOICE,
AND I KNOW THEM, AND THEY
FOLLOW ME.

JOHN 10:27

Today's verse continues the Good Shepherd metaphor of John 10. The Jews often did not understand why Jesus wasn't more forthright about His identity. They asked, "How long do You keep us in doubt? If You are the Christ, tell us plainly" (v. 24). Despite all of Jesus' miracles, many still weren't sure about Him. They wanted Him to tell them plainly He was the Messiah. Jesus responded: "I told you, and you do not believe. The works that I do in My Father's name, they bear witness of Me" (v. 25). Jesus had already proved His identity by His actions, and it still wasn't sufficient.

Next, Jesus told the crowd why they were so confused. These Jews were not His sheep. They didn't believe He was the Son of God, so they didn't recognize the Good Shepherd's voice. In contrast are the sheep Jesus mentioned in today's verse: those who are His sheep hear His voice and follow Him. He gives them eternal life, and no one will be able to snatch them out of His hand.

If you follow Jesus, then you are of His flock. Pray that you will heed the voice of your Good Shepherd and follow His guidance.

I AM

THE

RESURRECTION

AND THE | HE WHO

LIFE. | **BELIEVES**

IN ME,

THOUGH HE MAY DIE, HE SHALL

LIVE.

JOHN 11:25

Jesus heard Lazarus was sick, but He didn't immediately leave to be at the side of His friend. When Jesus arrived in Bethany, Lazarus had been dead for four days. Lazarus' sisters—Mary and Martha—knew Jesus could have healed their brother had He arrived in time.

Martha confronted Jesus after His arrival. Jesus assured Martha that Lazarus would rise again. She responded, "I know that he will rise again in the resurrection at the last day" (v. 24). Jesus then proclaimed: "I am the resurrection and the life." Those who believe in Him will have eternal life. Jesus asked Martha if she believed this, and she confessed He was the Son of God.

Mary also found Jesus and expressed her sorrow that Jesus had not come sooner. Upon seeing Mary's tears, Jesus also wept. Soon afterward, though, both sisters saw Jesus raise their brother from the dead. Undoubtedly their faith in Jesus' power grew exponentially.

God is sometimes more concerned with growing your faith than making you comfortable. When God appears to be taking His time, perhaps He is preparing to work a true miracle in your life.

IF ANYONE
SERVES *Me,* HIM MY
Father WILL HONOR.

JOHN 12:26

Throughout His ministry, Jesus emphasized being a servant. Prior to today's verse, Jesus told His disciples that if they wanted eternal life, then they must be willing to lose their lives in the eyes of the world. This meant they must be willing to put God's will first in everything they do—regardless of what it costs them. Part of losing their lives and following Jesus involves being a servant to others. As a result, the Father will honor His followers who serve others.

Jesus was the ultimate servant, and He humbled Himself by leaving the glories of heaven and taking on human flesh. When Jesus died on the cross, He yielded to His Father's will and, in doing so, served all of humanity by dying for our sins. Jesus' sacrificial death was an act of service on our behalf. In response to this service, we show our appreciation by serving God and serving others.

This kind of love means serving others, which means living for the betterment of others. In serving others, you serve Jesus, and the Father will honor you for your service.

AND I, if I am *lifted up* FROM THE EARTH, WILL *draw* ALL *peoples* to MYSELF.

John 12:32

Jesus' disciples did not always understand the meaning of His parables and figurative language, and sometimes further complicating the matter was the fact that Jesus' words had multiple meanings. The words of Jesus in John 12:32 are an example of this. First, in saying He would be lifted up, Jesus predicted His death where He would be lifted up on a cross. With that sacrificial death, Jesus draws to Himself people who are aware of their sin, recognize Jesus as God's Son and the perfect Lamb whose blood offers cleansing from their sin, and choose to serve Him as Savior, Lord, and King.

Second, Jesus referenced the future lifting up He would receive from the Father. After His death on the cross, Jesus rose from the dead and forty days later ascended to heaven. He currently sits at the right hand of the Father and thus is lifted up by the praise and honor due Him. On earth, His followers continue to draw people to Jesus by living in ways that exalt Him.

You should live in such a way that lifts Jesus up—honoring Him in your words and actions—so others will be drawn to your living Savior.

BELIEVE

IN THE

Light,

THAT YOU MAY

BECOME SONS OF LIGHT.

JOHN 12:36

Earlier in the Gospel of John, Jesus declared He was the Light of the world. He is the Light that reveals sin and points the way to salvation through His death on the cross and resurrection from the grave. Yet similar to people today, not everyone in Jesus' day recognized Him as the Light of the world.

The people Jesus spoke with in John 12:27–36 did not recognize He was the Son of God. After a voice from heaven spoke to vindicate Jesus' claim, the people attributed the voice to an angel or just thunder. In spite of this, Jesus once again invited His listeners to follow Him: "While you have the light, believe in the light, that you may become sons of light." Jesus knew the time was coming when His light would no longer shine in the world; the people needed to accept Him before it was too late.

Jesus wanted the people then—and He wants you today—to be children of the light, to believe in His teachings, obey His commands, follow His guidance, and rest in the truth that He is God's Son.

IF I THEN, YOUR

Lord & Teacher,

HAVE WASHED YOUR FEET,

YOU ALSO OUGHT TO

WASH ONE ANOTHER'S FEET.

JOHN 13:14

In biblical times, most people's feet were filthy from walking everywhere. Thus, showing hospitality to visitors included washing their feet. The lowest of servants usually had the task of washing the feet of those who entered the home.

But in the upper room in John 13, none of the disciples volunteered for that lowly duty.

This didn't stop Jesus from showing hospitality to His disciples. After dinner was over, Jesus arose, wrapped a towel around Himself, poured water in a basin, and began to wash the feet of His disciples. At first Peter balked at Jesus' trying to wash his feet, but Jesus explained all needed to be cleansed spiritually to have any part of Him.

Jesus' purpose in washing the disciples' feet was to show love and model servanthood. He demonstrated to His disciples that the Christian life requires the giving of oneself in service to others. This is true love in action.

Genuine faith and love should lead to godly action, and God uses your actions to bring others to Himself. Are you being a servant to others? If not, ask God to show whom you can serve.

A new commandment
I give to you,
that you

love one another;
as I have loved you,
that you also
love one another.

JOHN 13:34

For approximately fifty years Christians have sung the popular hymn "They'll Know We Are Christians." The song, written by Peter Scholtes, asserts the world will recognize Christians by the love that flows among believers. This hymn lines up with Jesus' command in today's verse: "Love one another." In doing this, His disciples could easily be identified as His followers.

Love should be the defining characteristic of Christians because God is love (1 John 4:8). This love was seen when He sent His Son to die for humanity. Thus, any follower of God should imitate this same love for others, especially brothers and sisters in Christ.

The world will not know you are His disciple by your correct doctrine or elaborate church building. Rather, the world will recognize you by your love for other believers.

Therefore, as you go through your daily activities, try to honor God with your loving actions in service of other Christians. In this way, the watching world will be able to identify you as a follower of Christ.

I WILL

come again

& **receive you to Myself;**

THAT WHERE I AM,

THERE YOU MAY BE ALSO.

JOHN 14:3

After the Last Supper, the disciples were understandably upset. Jesus had identified His betrayer, predicted Peter's denial, and then told His disciples that He would be leaving them soon. Recognizing their fears, Jesus spoke words of comfort in John 14–17, which Christians today commonly call the Farewell Discourse. Jesus began by telling the disciples, "Let not your heart be troubled" (John 14:1). Then He offered them hope: He was leaving to prepare a place for His disciples, and one day He would come back to take His disciples to be with Him.

Jesus gave no timetable for these events. He didn't offer specific details about the place He would prepare for His followers. But He did promise He would return for His people so "that where I am, there you may be also." The words Jesus spoke must have greatly comforted the disciples in their time of despair.

The words of comfort, the hope that Jesus will prepare a better place, and the promise of His returning to take His people to that place are also meant for you today.

I AM THE *way,*

THE *truth,*

AND THE *life.*

JOHN 14:6

This devotion continues Jesus' words of comfort to His disciples in John 14–17. The disciples knew Jesus would soon be gone, and they anticipated being with Jesus in the place He would prepare for them. But Jesus confused the disciples when He said they knew where He was going and how to get to that place. Thus, Thomas spoke up: "Lord, we do not know where You are going, and how can we know the way?" (v. 5). To this Jesus responded, "I am the way, the truth, and the life."

First, Jesus is the only way to the Father: "No one comes to the Father except through Me" (v. 6). No other way to heaven exists. Second, Jesus is the truth, which He made clear through His "I am" statements and through His actions to prove He was truly God's Son and the fulfillment of Old Testament prophecies. Finally, Jesus is the life, which was illustrated earlier when Jesus said to Martha, "Whoever lives and believes in Me shall never die" (John 11:26). Jesus' resurrection—His defeat of sin and death—guarantees eternal life for His followers.

Jesus' words have not changed. He remains the way, the truth, and the life for you today.

IF YOU HAD KNOWN

Me,

YOU WOULD HAVE KNOWN

My Father ALSO.

JOHN 14:7

As Jesus delivered His words of comfort to His disciples, He continued to reiterate the fact that He and the Father are one. Even though Jesus had just told His disciples this truth, Philip asked Jesus, "Lord, show us the Father" (v. 8).

Jesus had fed thousands, calmed a storm, healed people, and walked on water. Jesus had proclaimed His deity in multiple "I am" statements, and on occasion He specifically stated: "I and My Father are one" (John 10:30). Yet even in Jesus' final hours the disciples did not fully grasp that Jesus and the Father are one.

Jesus told Philip: "He who has seen Me has seen the Father" (John 14:9). The disciples had seen this truth illustrated time and time again in Jesus' ministry. Through His actions Jesus had illustrated His divinity. The words Jesus had spoken were the words the Father had given Him to speak. Thus, the disciples had no excuse for not recognizing Jesus was the Son of God and equal with the Father.

The same is true for Christians today. If you know Jesus, then you know His heavenly Father.

WHATEVER *you ask* IN *My Name,*

THAT I WILL DO, THAT THE

FATHER

MAY BE GLORIFIED

IN THE *Son.*

JOHN 14:13

Jesus told His disciples that whatever they asked in His name would be given to them. This is also a wonderful promise for you today. First, consider "ask in My name." Many Christians close their prayers with "in Jesus' name, amen." This is not a required closing or a phrase that ensures you will get what you asked for. Instead, praying in Jesus' name means praying according to God's will. Therefore, you can offer requests and be as specific and persistent as you wish, but if your requests are not aligned with God's will, you cannot expect Jesus to grant them.

Second, your prayer requests should have God's glory as the ultimate goal. You should not be focused on your comfort, success, recognition, or glory. Your prayers should not be focused on having a prestigious job or living in a rich neighborhood. Rather, your prayers should be about accomplishing God's will and giving Him glory. Your daily prayer should be "Your will be done on earth as it is in heaven" (Matthew 6:10).

If you follow these guidelines in prayer, then you will have a richer prayer life that is in accordance with God's will for your life.

HE WHO HAS

MY COMMANDMENTS

&

KEEPS THEM,

IT IS HE WHO

Loves Me.

JOHN 14:21

In John 15, Jesus gave another "I am" statement in which He identified Himself as the vine and specified what your relationship with Him needs to be if you are to bear fruit for His kingdom.

Water and nutrients for a plant flow through the vine to the branches. Apart from the vine, the tree's branches cannot survive, much less bear fruit. In fact, the branches are productive only insofar as the vine is healthy and their connection to the vine is strong.

What did Jesus mean when He called Himself the vine and His followers the branches? The only way you can play a significant role in the kingdom of God is to allow Jesus to live in you and work through you. Jesus warned His disciples, "Without Me you can do nothing" (v. 5), meaning His disciples could accomplish nothing of lasting spiritual value without His help.

This leads to a warning from Jesus: those who do not bear good fruit will be cast off and thrown into the fire (v. 6). If you want to bear fruit that will last into eternity, you need to be attached to His vine.

GREATER

HAS NO ONE
THAN THIS,

THAN TO LAY DOWN ONE'S

LIFE FOR HIS FRIENDS.

JOHN 15:13

In an epistle he wrote to the early church, John plainly stated: "God is love" (1 John 4:8). Love is a central part of God's nature. Because of His great love, God pursued a relationship with sinners even at the cost of His Son's life. This great love also prompted Jesus to submit to that plan. And that plan—dying on the cross for your sins—is what Jesus talked about in today's verse.

What could be a greater demonstration of love "than to lay down one's life for his friends"? Jesus willingly dying on the cross for the sins of the world is the greatest act of love the world has ever known. Jesus did this because He loves everyone and wants to see all come to salvation.

Further, this great act cements your friendship with Him. As your friend, Jesus visits with you, converses with you, bears your burdens, and pleads for you on your behalf. He also models for you a life of service, sacrificial love, and laying down your life for your friends. He wants you to go and share that loving friendship with others.

I chose YOU AND *appointed* YOU THAT YOU SHOULD GO AND BEAR

FRUIT.

JOHN 15:16

Everyone wants to belong to a group, to feel valued, to be chosen—and Jesus said to His disciples, "I chose you." Jesus' words apply to you today as well. He has chosen you to be His friend and—at the same time—a worker in His kingdom.

Jesus does not want you to lead an unproductive life as His follower. Therefore, He chose you not only for salvation, but also to play a significant role in building His kingdom. You are to share the good news of Jesus' love and forgiveness around the world. You are to love people with His love. You are to be salt in the world, preserving goodness until Jesus returns. You are to be a light in the world, shining the light of God's truth and His ways. You are to serve in your family, church, neighborhood, and workplace as if you were serving Jesus Himself. In these ways and others—in acts big and small, seen and unseen—you are to bear fruit that glorifies God and draws people into His family.

WHEN HE,
the *Spirit*
of *truth,*
HAS COME,
HE WILL GUIDE YOU
JOHN 16:13
INTO ALL TRUTH.

Jesus knew His time with His disciples was limited, yet He still had much to say. Recognizing the disciples could not handle all He had to tell them, Jesus explained the Holy Spirit would come and "guide [His disciples] into all truth" and help them in the days that lay ahead.

Notice that word *guide*. The Holy Spirit will not control you or force you. The Holy Spirit's guidance will instead help you discover what is true about God. This is especially applicable when it comes to understanding the truth of God's Word. The Holy Spirit guides you in interpreting the Scriptures correctly and applying them to your life.

Guided by the Holy Spirit, you can learn—and continue to learn—what is wise and what is foolish. The Holy Spirit never speaks on His own authority. Just like the Son, the Holy Spirit willingly submits to the authority of the Father when speaking to the hearts and minds of believers. Therefore, the Holy Spirit works in conjunction with the will of the Father.

Open your heart to the guidance of the Holy Spirit. He will never lead you down the wrong path.

IN THE WORLD
YOU *will* HAVE
TRIBULATION;
BUT BE OF GOOD CHEER,
I HAVE
overcome
THE WORLD.

JOHN 16:33

If you were to read the news headlines, you might infer that no one is in control of worldwide events, yet those who love the Lord know otherwise. Today's verse speaks of God's sovereign power over evil. After acknowledging His disciples would experience great tribulation, Jesus told them not to fear because He had "overcome the world."

Jesus knew the disciples were about to face life without Him and would endure persecution for His name's sake. In fact, all of them, excluding John, would eventually give their lives furthering the gospel message. Likewise, Christians today still face pain and suffering due to persecution or disease or broken relationships.

Yet God graciously uses suffering to compel you to lean into Him, to grow and refine your faith, to receive His comfort, and to keep your eyes on heaven. Yes, you will experience heartache, disappointment, unfairness, and outright evil in the world, but do not despair because Jesus has overcome this world. When going through tribulation, you can take comfort in the promise of "a new heaven and a new earth. . . . [where] there shall be no more pain" (Revelation 21:1, 4).

I HAVE GLORIFIED YOU ON THE EARTH.

I HAVE FINISHED THE

WORK

WHICH YOU HAVE GIVEN ME TO DO.

JOHN 17:4

John 17 contains Jesus' High Priestly Prayer. In this prayer, offered just before His crucifixion, Jesus prayed first for Himself. Then He prayed for His disciples, as well as those who will follow Him in the future. Such a prayer illustrates the love Jesus had for His followers; in His darkest hour, He prayed for others rather than just Himself.

At the beginning of His prayer, Jesus asked the Father to "Glorify Your Son, that Your Son also may glorify You" (v. 1). Jesus was determined to fulfill the task that lay ahead of Him. He chose to submit to the will of His Father in spite of the pain and suffering He would endure.

Acknowledging that the end of His earthly ministry was at hand, Jesus told the Father, "I have glorified You on the earth." For three years, Jesus had ministered to bring glory to His Father. This ministry would soon culminate in Jesus' serving as the perfect sacrifice for all of humanity's sins, an act that would bring glory to the Father.

Live in such a way that brings glory to the Father just as the Son sought to glorify the Father.

I pray for . . .

THOSE WHOM

YOU

HAVE
GIVEN *Me,*

for they are Yours.

JOHN 17:9

In the second part of Jesus' High Priestly Prayer, Jesus prayed for His disciples, the men who had spent the last three years traveling with Him. Acknowledging that each man in this circle of support was a gift to Him from God, Jesus praised the Father for giving Him these disciples who had believed His words and followed Him.

Jesus knew the disciples didn't fully understand what lay in store for them. This included the next few days of heartache and confusion, the Holy Spirit's coming on Pentecost, and their taking the gospel to the ends of the earth, even at the risk of death. But Jesus knew what awaited His disciples, so He prayed for them, taking them before the throne of God with specific requests: "keep them from the evil one" (v. 15) and "sanctify them by Your truth" (v. 17). Jesus prayed God would protect them and set them apart for His service.

What a precious glimpse into the prayers Jesus prays for those whom He loves. In similar fashion, you are blessed to have Jesus, the great High Priest, still standing at the right hand of the Father in heaven and interceding for you.

FATHER, I DESIRE

that they also

WHOM YOU GAVE ME

may be

 with Me

WHERE I AM.

JOHN 17:24

In the final part of Jesus' High Priestly Prayer—His final recorded prayer before He went to the cross—Jesus prayed for all future believers, "for those who will believe in Me" (v. 20). First, Jesus prayed for unity among believers, and then He asked that these believers would help "the world . . . believe that You sent Me" (v. 21). If Christians unify together, then their efforts to spread the gospel will be much more successful.

Jesus also longed for believers to see the glory God had given Him as His Son. He wanted them to witness the glory of His majesty. Jesus' words also reveal the great love He has for His followers: "I desire that they also whom You gave Me may be with Me where I am." Thus, Jesus wants His followers to be with Him throughout all eternity.

Perhaps you don't always understand what Jesus is doing in your life, don't always go where He leads you, or don't always display your faith in Him—yet He never stops loving and caring for you.

In Jesus' final hours on earth, you were on His mind.

As the Father
has sent

ME,
I also send

YOU.

John 20:21

After the crucifixion the disciples greatly feared for their safety. Their Lord had been arrested, falsely condemned, and killed. A similar fate seemed likely to befall each of them, so hiding together behind locked doors seemed wise. Then the narrative changed: "Jesus came and stood in the midst" (v. 19). This appearance by Jesus must have shocked the disciples. No wonder Jesus' first words to them were "Peace be with you!" (v.19).

The Scriptures clearly state the Father sent His Son into the world to make it possible for sinful men and women to be forgiven and welcomed into the family of God. Now the risen Son commissioned His disciples to go into the world to tell others that Jesus conquered sin and death. To fortify His disciples against evil and prepare for the task ahead, Jesus breathed on them and gave them a foretaste of Pentecost when the Spirit would descend in full (Acts 2).

The disciples' commission to share God's truth is your commission as well, and the same Holy Spirit will empower you, both for the good of your listeners and God's glory.

DO NOT BE
UNbelieving,
BUT believing.

John 20:27

John 20:24–29, the closing scene in John's Gospel, opens with informing the reader that Thomas was not present when Jesus had appeared to the disciples after His resurrection. When Thomas heard about that amazing event, he said he would not believe Jesus was alive unless he could touch His hands, His feet, and His side.

Eight days later Jesus gave Thomas the opportunity to keep his word. Jesus suddenly appeared in the midst of the disciples once again. He told Thomas, "Reach your finger here, and look at My hands; and reach your hand here, and put it into My side. Do not be unbelieving, but believing" (v. 27). Thomas had no trouble believing, answering simply, "My Lord and my God!" (v. 28). Thomas knew that He had just seen the risen Christ.

This scene closes with a benediction. Jesus said, "Blessed are those who have not seen and yet have believed" (v. 29). True faith requires trusting in Jesus even when you cannot touch and see Him. This is what Jesus requires of you to be His follower. If you will place your total trust in Jesus, then you shall receive the blessing of salvation.

215

Behold,
I stand
at the door
& *knock.*

REVELATION 3:20

In the book of Revelation Jesus encouraged believers to continue where they were strong and challenged them to strengthen their weaknesses. Today's verse comes from Jesus' words to the church in Laodicea. He spoke directly and forcefully: "You are neither cold nor hot. . . . So then, because you are lukewarm, and neither cold nor hot, I will vomit you out of My mouth" (vv. 15–16).

More frank words followed: "As many as I love, I rebuke and chasten" (v. 19). Just as a father disciplines his child, so Jesus disciplines believers who need correction. Jesus called His people to repentance: "Behold, I stand at the door and knock. If anyone hears My voice and opens the door, I will come in to him and dine with him, and he with Me" (v. 20). Those in the Laodicean church who repented would receive forgiveness of sin and renewed fellowship with Him.

Jesus longs to be in an intimate relationship with you as well. Will you open the door?

us said to him, "You shall love the Lord you

h all your mind." —Matthew 22:37   Jesus sa

your heart, with all your soul, and with all

n shall love the Lord your God with all your

Matthew 22:37   Jesus said to him, "You shal

your soul, and with all your mind."   —Matth

d your God with all your heart, with all you

us said to him, "You shall love the Lord you

h all your mind."   —Matthew 22:37   Jesus sa

your heart, with all your soul, and with all

n shall love the Lord your God with all your

Matthew 22:37   Jesus said to him, "You shal

your soul, and with all your mind."   —Matth

d your God with all your heart, with all you